Better Homes and Gardens®
Dessert Cook Book

Contents

On the cover: Upside-Down Berry Meringue Pie *satisfies anyone's dessert appetite with its hidden meringue under fresh strawberry filling and sweet whipped cream topper. (See recipe, page 40.)*

To the left: *Serve guests generous wedges of* Chocolate Cheesecake Torte. *It features a mandarin orange-dotted cheesecake filling between luscious chocolate cake layers. (See recipe, page 24.)*

BETTER HOMES AND GARDENS BOOKS

Editorial Director: Don Dooley
Managing Editor: Malcolm E. Robinson   Art Director: John Berg
Asst. Managing Editor: Lawrence D. Clayton   Asst. Art Director: Randall Yontz
Food Editor: Nancy Morton
Senior Food Editor: Joyce Trollope
Associate Editors: Sharyl Heiken, Rosemary Corsiglia
Assistant Editors: Sandra Mapes, Elizabeth Strait
Designers: Harijs Priekulis, Tonya Rodriguez
Contributing Editor: Pat Olson

Desserts for Everyone

Are you bamboozled by baked Alaska, chary of making a cheesecake, or pie-shy of pastry? If you said yes to any of the above, you are missing some of the greatest fun in cooking—the making and serving of fancy desserts. You can get in on the enjoyment and the compliments by preparing these and other appealing treats from the pages of the *Dessert Cook Book*.

Although emphasis throughout the book is on desserts with dazzle, those in the opening section are unabashed show-offs. Here, for example, are the flaming desserts, the crepes, the soufflés. Some are difficult, while others are deceptively easy to make. All start with tested recipes you can follow with confidence.

Happy endings for family meals are features of the recipe collection in the Dessert Treasury. Cakes of all kinds, with variations such as the luscious *Strawberry Meringue Cake* pictured opposite (see recipe, page 71), are followed by an array of pies in pastry and crumb crusts. Satisfying puddings, enticing cookies, and homey fruit concoctions also are included. Special tip boxes here, as elsewhere, answer many how-to questions. Calorie-counted recipes are flagged for quick identification.

Not enough time to make desserts? This problem gets double-barreled treatment in the final section. The first is by taking shortcuts with the recipes. These may be through the use of convenience products, or timesaving techniques, or both. The second approach is to make ahead, that is to actually prepare the dessert a day or more before you need it. The refrigerator or freezer takes over storage duties.

Answers to that old question, "What's for dessert," come in a myriad of shapes, sizes, colors, and flavor combinations. All are delectable to eat and await your creative touch in the kitchen.

The Editors

Our seal assures you that every recipe in the *Dessert Cook Book* is endorsed by the Better Homes and Gardens Test Kitchen. Each recipe is thoroughly tested for family appeal, practicality, and deliciousness.

Spectacular Desserts

Turn dessert time into a memorable occasion. Select from this chapter of recipes designed to add glamour to family or entertaining situations. This dazzling array of desserts includes Chocolate Mint Torte, Fresh Pineapple Jubilee, Chocolate-Pecan Cornucopias, Vanilla Éclairs, and Soufflé Grand Marnier. (See index for page numbers.)

Flame a Dessert

Apricot Cream Fondue

Equally delicious with gingerbread cubes—

        1 30-ounce can unpeeled apricot
           halves, drained
    ⅓ cup sugar
        1 tablespoon cornstarch
    ¾ cup whipping cream
        1 tablespoon lemon juice
           Pound cake cubes
           Angel cake cubes
           Apple slices
           Banana slices

Blend apricots in blender till smooth, or press through a sieve or food mill. In fondue cooker combine sugar and cornstarch. Stir in apricot purée, cream, and lemon juice. Cook and stir till thickened and bubbly. Place over fondue burner. Spear cake cubes or fruit pieces with fondue fork and dip into fondue, swirling to coat. Makes 6 to 8 servings.

Apple Fritter Fondue

Set several bowls of sugar and cinnamon on the table for dipping the fried morsels—

        1 cup pancake mix
    ⅔ cup milk
        1 egg
        1 tablespoon cooking oil
    ½ cup sugar
        2 teaspoons ground cinnamon
           Cooking oil
        4 medium apples, peeled, cored,
           and sliced

Combine first 4 ingredients. Beat till smooth. Combine sugar and cinnamon; pour into small bowls or shakers. Pour cooking oil into fondue cooker to no more than ½ capacity or to depth of 2 inches. Heat over range to 375°. Transfer cooker to fondue burner. Spear apple with fondue fork; dip into batter. Fry in hot oil till golden brown, 1 to 2 minutes. Sprinkle with sugar-cinnamon mixture. Makes 6 servings.

Cranberry Jubilee

    ¼ cup sugar
        2 teaspoons cornstarch
    ½ teaspoon ground cinnamon
    ¼ teaspoon ground nutmeg
           Dash ground cloves
        1 16-ounce can whole cranberry
           sauce
    ¼ cup brandy
           Vanilla ice cream

In saucepan combine sugar, cornstarch, and spices. Blend in cranberry sauce and 2 table-spoons water. Cook and stir till thickened and bubbly. Stir in *1 tablespoon* of the brandy. Turn into chafing dish or heatproof bowl. Heat remaining brandy in ladle or small pan just till warm; flame and pour over cranberry mixture. Blend into sauce and serve immediately over ice cream. Makes 2 cups sauce.

Fresh Pineapple Jubilee

This festive dessert is shown on pages 6 and 7—

    ½ cup orange marmalade
        2 tablespoons packed brown sugar
        2 tablespoons light corn syrup
        2 cups diced pineapple
    ¼ cup orange-flavored liqueur
           Vanilla ice cream

Combine orange marmalade, brown sugar, and corn syrup in blazer pan of chafing dish; stir in pineapple. Cook and stir over direct heat till warm. Heat liqueur in small pan; flame and pour over pineapple mixture. Mix into sauce. Serve over ice cream. Makes 2 cups.

Exciting tabletop dessert finale

Pass fondue forks and offer angel cake cubes, →
pound cake cubes, apple slices, and banana chunks
for dunking in smooth Apricot Cream Fondue.

Enjoy an Éclair

Basic Éclairs

½ cup butter or margarine
1 cup boiling water
1 cup all-purpose flour
¼ teaspoon salt
4 eggs

In saucepan melt butter in boiling water. Add flour and salt all at once; stir vigorously. Cook and stir till mixture forms a ball that doesn't separate. Remove from heat; cool slightly. Add eggs, one at a time; beat after each addition till smooth. Shape on greased baking sheet as directed in recipe. Bake at 400° till golden and puffy, 30 to 35 minutes. Remove from oven; split. Cool on rack.

Vanilla Éclairs

These special éclairs are shown on pages 6 and 7 —

Basic Éclairs
1 3- or 3¼-ounce package regular
   vanilla pudding mix
1½ cups milk
1 cup whipping cream
¼ teaspoon vanilla
Sifted powdered sugar
1 slightly beaten egg white
Small multicolored decorative
   candies

Prepare Basic Éclair dough. Put through a pastry tube or spread with spoon, making strips 4x1½ inches on greased baking sheet. Bake and cool as directed in Basic Éclairs.

For filling prepare pudding mix according to package directions, *except* use the 1½ cups milk instead of the liquid called for. Chill thoroughly. Whip cream to stiff peaks. Beat pudding smooth; fold in whipped cream and vanilla. Fill éclairs with pudding mixture. Stir enough powdered sugar (about 1¼ cups) into egg white to make of spreading consistency. Frost tops of éclairs. Sprinkle with candies. Chill till served. Makes 10.

Coffee-Ice Cream Éclairs

Basic Éclairs
1 quart vanilla or coffee ice cream
1 cup light corn syrup
1½ cups water
1 tablespoon instant coffee powder
3 tablespoons cornstarch
2 tablespoons butter or margarine
1 teaspoon vanilla
½ cup chopped pecans

Prepare Basic Éclair dough. Using about ¼ cup dough for each éclair, drop from spoon onto greased baking sheet 2 inches apart, leaving 6 inches between rows. Shape each mound into a 4x1-inch rectangle, rounding sides and piling dough on top. Bake and cool as directed in Basic Éclairs recipe.

Fill bottom halves of éclairs with vanilla or coffee ice cream; replace tops. Keep in freezer till serving time.

Meanwhile, to make sauce, measure corn syrup into saucepan. Combine water and coffee powder; blend in cornstarch. Stir into syrup in pan. Cook and stir till thickened and bubbly. Remove from heat; add butter and vanilla. Stir till butter melts; stir in pecans. Serve warm sauce over éclairs. Makes 10 to 12.

Cream puff tips

Éclairs and cream puffs are made from the same dough. They are just shaped differently. For cream puffs, prepare the Basic Éclair dough. Drop the dough by rounded tablespoons onto a greased baking sheet. Bake at 400° till golden brown and puffy, about 30 minutes. Split; cool on rack. Fill with your favorite filling.

For a crisp, hollow puff, remove the excess center membrane from each puff before cooling.

Dazzling Banana Split Éclairs appeal to dessert lovers of all ages. A puffy, golden éclair holds all the classic banana split ingredients: refreshing ice creams, ripe bananas, luscious toppings, and chopped nuts.

Banana Split Éclairs

A luscious variation of an old-fashioned treat—

Basic Éclairs
6 small bananas, sliced
Strawberry-Macaroon Ice Cream
Sherry-Vanilla Ice Cream
Chocolate-Almond Ice Cream

• • •

Strawberry ice cream topping
Caramel ice cream topping
Pineapple ice cream topping
Chopped nuts

Prepare Basic Éclair dough. Spoon dough into pastry bag with a ¾-inch round tube opening. Squeeze the dough onto a greased baking sheet in six strips, 5½x1¾ inches each. Bake and cool as directed in Basic Éclairs recipe.

Fill each éclair with a sliced banana and a small scoop each of Strawberry-Macaroon Ice Cream, Sherry-Vanilla Ice Cream, and Chocolate-Almond Ice Cream. Ladle strawberry, caramel, and pineapple ice cream toppings over. Garnish with chopped nuts. Cover with top of éclair, if desired. Makes 6 servings.

Strawberry-Macaroon Ice Cream: In chilled bowl quickly soften 1 pint strawberry ice cream; stir in ½ cup crumbled soft coconut macaroons and return to freezer immediately.

Sherry-Vanilla Ice Cream: In chilled bowl quickly soften 1 pint vanilla ice cream; stir in 1 tablespoon cream sherry. Return mixture to freezer immediately.

Chocolate-Almond Ice Cream: In chilled bowl quickly soften 1 pint chocolate ice cream; stir in ¼ cup sliced, toasted almonds. Return mixture to freezer immediately.

More Pastries to Savor

Napoleons

    1 cup chilled butter or margarine
1¾ cups all-purpose flour
  ½ cup ice water
  1 slightly beaten egg white
  1 tablespoon ice water
    Napoleon Filling
    Vanilla Glaze
    Chocolate Icing

Set aside *2 tablespoons* butter; chill. Work remaining butter with back of wooden spoon or in electric mixer *just till* pliable. Roll or pat between two sheets of waxed paper to 8x6-inch rectangle. Chill thoroughly, at least 1 hour in refrigerator or 20 minutes in freezer. Keep utensils cold; chill before each use.

Cut reserved 2 tablespoons butter into flour with pastry blender till mixture resembles coarse meal. Gradually add ½ cup ice water, tossing with fork to make stiff dough. Shape into ball. Turn onto lightly floured surface; knead till smooth and elastic, about 5 minutes. Cover; let rest 10 minutes.

On lightly floured surface, roll dough to 15x9-inch rectangle. Remove top sheet of waxed paper from chilled rectangle of butter; invert butter over half the pastry. Remove waxed paper. Fold pastry over butter, sealing edges by pressing with heel of hand. Wrap in waxed paper; chill thoroughly, at least 1 hour in refrigerator or 20 minutes in freezer.

Unwrap. On lightly floured surface, roll to 15x9-inch rectangle, starting from center and rolling just to the edges. (Do not flatten edges by rolling them—pastry should be even thickness.) Brush excess flour from pastry. Fold dough in thirds; then turn and fold in thirds again. (Pastry now has 9 layers.) Seal edges with heel of hand. Wrap in waxed paper; chill thoroughly. Repeat rolling, folding, and chilling 2 more times.

Roll to 14x8-inch rectangle. With floured sharp knife, cut off edges. Prick dough thoroughly with fork. Cut in sixteen 3½x2-inch rectangles. Cover baking sheets with 3 or 4 thicknesses of paper toweling; place pastry rectangles on toweling. Chill thoroughly. Combine egg white and 1 tablespoon ice water; brush over pastry. (Do not remove toweling.) Bake at 450° for 6 minutes. Reduce temperature to 300°; bake till lightly browned and crisp, 25 to 30 minutes more. Remove from baking sheets; cool on rack. Separate each pastry into 3 layers. Fill between layers with Napoleon Filling; spread top with Vanilla Glaze. Drizzle Chocolate Icing over. Makes 16.

Napoleon Filling: In saucepan combine 1 cup sugar, ¼ cup all-purpose flour, ¼ cup cornstarch, and ½ teaspoon salt. Stir in 3 cups milk. Cook and stir till thickened and bubbly. Stir a little of the hot mixture into 4 beaten egg yolks; return to hot mixture in saucepan. Cook and stir just till boiling. Cool; stir in 2 teaspoons vanilla. Chill. Beat smooth just before filling Napoleons.

Vanilla Glaze: Mix 2 cups sifted powdered sugar, ¼ teaspoon vanilla, and dash salt. Beat in enough boiling water (2 to 3 tablespoons) to make of spreading consistency.

Chocolate Icing: Melt together one 1-ounce square unsweetened chocolate and 1 teaspoon butter. Cool. Stir in 3 tablespoons sifted powdered sugar and dash salt; mix smooth. Stir in enough boiling water (about 4 teaspoons) to make of spreading consistency.

Lemon-Filled Cream Puffs

    Basic Éclairs (see recipe, page 10)
  1 18-ounce can lemon pudding
  ½ cup dairy sour cream
  ½ cup whipping cream

Prepare Basic Éclair dough. Drop by rounded tablespoonfuls onto greased baking sheet. Bake at 400° till golden brown and puffy, about 30 minutes. Split; cool on rack.

For filling, stir together pudding and sour cream. Whip cream; fold into pudding mixture. Chill. Just before serving, fill cream puffs with pudding mixture. Makes 10.

Cherry-Filled Cream Puffs

In saucepan crumble 1 stick piecrust mix into ½ cup boiling water; cook and stir vigorously till pastry forms ball and leaves sides of pan. Cook and stir 1 minute more over low heat. Remove from heat. Add 2 eggs, one at a time; beat at low speed of electric mixer for 1 minute after each. Drop about 3 tablespoons mixture for each puff onto greased baking sheet. Bake at 400° till golden and puffy, 30 to 35 minutes. Remove from sheet; cool on rack.

Cut off tops of cream puffs; remove excess webbing. Set aside ½ *cup* of one 21-ounce can chilled cherry pie filling. Fold 2 cups frozen whipped dessert topping, thawed, and ½ cup flaked coconut into remaining cherry pie filling. Fill cream puffs, using about ½ cup pie filling mixture for each. Cover with tops of cream puffs; spoon reserved cherry pie filling over filled puffs. Makes 8 puffs.

Chocolate-Pecan Cornucopias

These pastry cones (shown on page 7) are filled with a chocolate- and coffee-flavored mixture—

Prepare 2 sticks piecrust mix according to package directions. Roll to a 16x12-inch rectangle. Cut into twelve 4-inch squares with pastry wheel. Overlap each to form a cone. For each, fold a 12-inch square of foil in quarters; shape into a cone. Insert in pastry cornucopias. Place on baking sheet; bake at 425° till golden brown, 10 to 12 minutes. Remove foil; cool cornucopias on rack.

Meanwhile, in mixer bowl combine 1 cup whipping cream, ¼ cup sugar, and 1 teaspoon instant coffee crystals, crushed. Stir till blended. Whip mixture till stiff. Fold in ½ cup grated sweet baking chocolate and ¼ cup finely chopped pecans. Pipe whipped cream-chocolate mixture into cornucopias. Garnish with pecan halves. Makes 12 servings.

Elegant Napoleons taste as delicious as they look. Sandwiched between the flaky layers is an unbelievably creamy vanilla filling. A sweet sugar glaze and chocolate icing further enhance this mouth-watering dessert.

Create a Crepe

Crepes Suzette

Serve these exquisite thin pancakes in orange sauce and flame with brandy —

    2 eggs
    ½ cup all-purpose flour
    ¾ cup milk
    1½ tablespoons sugar
    ¼ teaspoon vanilla
       Dash salt
       Shortening
         • • •
    ¼ cup butter or margarine
    ¼ cup orange-flavored liqueur
    ¼ cup orange juice
    3 tablespoons sugar
         • • •
    2 tablespoons brandy

With rotary beater beat together eggs, flour, milk, 1½ tablespoons sugar, vanilla, and salt. Heat heavy 6-inch skillet till a drop of water dances on it. Brush skillet lightly with shortening. Pour in about 2 tablespoons batter. Lift skillet and tilt from side to side till batter covers bottom. Cook till bottom of crepe is lightly browned and top appears dry, about 1½ minutes; turn out on paper toweling. Repeat with remaining batter.

In chafing dish combine butter or margarine, orange-flavored liqueur, orange juice, and 3 tablespoons sugar; heat till bubbly. Fold each crepe in quarters, browned side out, and arrange in sauce. Simmer till sauce thickens slightly, basting crepes frequently.

Warm brandy in small saucepan *just till hot.* Do not bring to boiling. Ignite and pour flaming brandy over crepes and orange sauce. Serve immediately. Makes 4 servings.

Glamorous fruit and crepe treat

← *Drizzle warm strawberry glaze over delicate crepes, plump with strawberries and served with banana quarters, to make* Curacao-Strawberry Crepes.

Curacao-Strawberry Crepes

Curacao, a tart, orange-flavored liqueur, accents the strawberry glaze —

    1 egg
    1¼ cups milk
    1¼ cups all-purpose flour
    1 tablespoon butter or margarine,
       melted
    ½ teaspoon salt
       Shortening
         • • • •
       Strawberry Glaze
    1 cup strawberries, sliced
    1 cup strawberries, halved
    3 medium bananas, quartered

Beat egg just to blend. Add milk, all-purpose flour, melted butter or margarine, and salt; beat mixture with rotary beater till smooth. Lightly grease an 8-inch skillet with shortening. Heat skillet; remove from heat and pour in ¼ cup batter. Quickly tilt pan from side to side till batter covers bottom. Return to heat; brown crepe on one side only. Turn out on paper toweling. Repeat with remaining batter to make 8 crepes. Stack crepes with 2 sheets of waxed paper between for easy separation.

Prepare Strawberry Glaze. Set aside 1 cup of the glaze; stir the 1 cup sliced strawberries into the remaining strawberry glaze. Spread *about 3 tablespoons glaze with berries* on unbrowned side of *each* crepe. Roll up. Place filled crepes in chafing dish or 10-inch skillet with the 1 cup strawberry halves and the quartered bananas. Pour the reserved Strawberry Glaze over; cover and heat through. Keep warm till ready to serve. Makes 8 servings.

Strawberry Glaze: In medium saucepan crush 2 cups strawberries; add ¾ cup water. Bring strawberry mixture to boiling; reduce heat and cook 2 minutes. Sieve. In saucepan combine ½ cup sugar and 2 tablespoons cornstarch; gradually stir in hot sieved strawberry mixture. Cook over medium heat, stirring constantly, till mixture thickens and bubbles. Remove from heat; stir in ⅓ cup curacao.

Bake an Alaska or Soufflé

Brownie Alaska

Cut the baked Alaska into thick slices, then halve them for serving-size pieces—

¼ cup butter or margarine, softened
1 cup sugar
2 egg yolks
¼ cup milk
½ teaspoon vanilla
2 1-ounce squares unsweetened
    chocolate, melted and cooled
• • •
⅔ cup all-purpose flour
½ teaspoon baking powder
½ teaspoon salt
2 stiffly beaten egg whites
⅓ cup chopped pecans
• • •
5 egg whites
⅔ cup sugar
2 pints coffee ice cream
¼ cup chopped pecans

In mixing bowl cream together butter or margarine and the 1 cup sugar till mixture is light and fluffy. Add egg yolks, milk, and vanilla; beat well. Stir in melted chocolate.

Stir together thoroughly flour, baking powder, and salt; add to creamed chocolate mixture in bowl. Mix well. Fold in 2 stiffly beaten egg whites. Turn mixture into greased and waxed paper-lined 9x9x2-inch baking pan. Sprinkle top with the ⅓ cup chopped pecans. Bake at 350° till done, 20 to 25 minutes. Remove from pan and cool on rack. Trim brownie layer to a 9x5-inch rectangle.

Beat the 5 egg whites till soft peaks form. Gradually add the ⅔ cup sugar; beat till stiff peaks form. Set meringue aside.

Place brownie rectangle on a *wooden board;* top with coffee ice cream, leaving a little of the brownie uncovered on all sides. Spread evenly with meringue, sealing carefully to brownie layer. Sprinkle top with remaining ¼ cup chopped pecans. Bake at 450° till meringue is lightly browned, about 5 minutes. Serve immediately. Makes 8 to 10 servings.

Soufflé Grand Marnier

This superb dessert is shown on page 6—

Butter or margarine
Granulated sugar
¼ cup all-purpose flour
¼ cup granulated sugar
¼ cup butter or margarine, softened
1 cup milk
5 egg yolks
2 tablespoons grand marnier
5 egg whites
¼ cup granulated sugar
Sifted powdered sugar

Lightly butter a 1½-quart soufflé dish; dust with a little granulated sugar to coat. Add foil collar, if desired. (Measure foil to go around dish; fold in thirds lengthwise. Butter well; sprinkle with more granulated sugar. With sugared side toward center, put collar around top, extending 2 inches above dish; fasten securely with tape.)

In small mixing bowl stir together thoroughly the all-purpose flour, ¼ cup granulated sugar, and the ¼ cup softened butter or margarine to make a smooth paste.

In saucepan heat milk to boiling; immediately remove from heat and add butter-flour mixture. Return to heat and cook and stir 2 minutes. Transfer mixture to mixing bowl. Add egg yolks, one at a time, beating well after each. Stir in grand marnier.

Beat egg whites till foamy; continue beating to stiff peaks, gradually adding the remaining ¼ cup granulated sugar. Fold yolk mixture into whites; turn into soufflé dish. Dust top heavily with powdered sugar. Bake at 400° for 30 to 35 minutes. Makes 8 servings.

Hot and cold pleasure treat

Rich coffee ice cream stays cool while the fluffy →
meringue is browned. The magical Brownie Alaska starts with a magnificent baked chocolate base.

Serve a Cake

Gateau Almond with Buttercream

½ cup unsalted butter
6 slightly beaten eggs
1 cup sugar
1 cup all-purpose flour
½ teaspoon vanilla
½ teaspoon almond extract
   Apricot Glaze
   Coffee Buttercream

Melt butter; set aside to cool. In bowl combine eggs and sugar; stir till just combined. Set bowl over large saucepan containing 2 inches hot, not boiling, water. Heat over low heat, stirring occasionally, till lukewarm, 8 to 10 minutes. Remove from heat. Beat at high speed of electric mixer till light and tripled in volume, about 15 minutes. Gently fold in flour, one-third at a time. Gradually fold in butter, vanilla, and almond extract. Pour into 2 greased and floured 9x1½-inch round baking pans. Bake at 350° till done, 25 to 30 minutes. Cool in pans 10 minutes; remove and cool.

To assemble cake, place one cake layer on piece of well-buttered waxed paper. Pour on hot Apricot Glaze. Transfer to cake platter. Place second cake layer atop first. Frost with Coffee Buttercream. Chill cake. If desired, pipe extra Coffee Buttercream through pastry tube over top of cake, and garnish with snipped candied apricots. Makes 12 servings.

Apricot Glaze: Mix and boil ½ cup sieved apricot preserves and 1 tablespoon brandy.

Coffee Buttercream: Beat 4 egg yolks till thick and lemon-colored; set aside. Cream 1 cup softened unsalted butter till fluffy; set aside. Combine ⅔ cup sugar, ¼ cup water, and 1 tablespoon instant coffee powder; bring to a boil, stirring to dissolve. Cook over medium-low heat, without stirring, to soft-ball stage (236°). Quickly pour hot syrup in steady stream into egg yolks, beating constantly at high speed of electric mixer. Continue beating till thick and smooth; cool. Beat in butter, a tablespoon at a time. Cover; chill till firm enough to spread, about 30 minutes.

Chocolate Malted Cheesecake

Creamy-smooth cheesecake sports a chocolate malt crust and a crumb topping—

1 cup all-purpose flour
⅓ cup chocolate-flavored malted milk
   powder
¼ teaspoon baking powder
¼ teaspoon salt
6 tablespoons butter or margarine
2 tablespoons sugar
   • • •
1 8-ounce package cream cheese,
   softened
1 cup small curd cream-style
   cottage cheese
½ cup sugar
2 eggs
2 teaspoons vanilla
2 tablespoons all-purpose flour
1 cup milk

To make crust, stir together thoroughly 1 cup all-purpose flour, malted milk powder, baking powder, and salt. Cream together butter or margarine and 2 tablespoons sugar till light and fluffy. Blend malt mixture into creamed mixture. Set aside ¼ cup crumb mixture. Press remaining into bottom and 1½ inches up side of *ungreased* 9-inch springform pan. Bake at 350° for 15 to 20 minutes. Bake the reserved ¼ cup crumb mixture on baking sheet for 8 to 10 minutes. Cool crust and crumbs.

In mixer bowl cream together softened cream cheese and cream-style cottage cheese till smooth. Gradually add the ½ cup sugar, creaming well. Add the eggs and vanilla; beat at low speed of electric mixer just till blended. Stir in the 2 tablespoons flour. Add milk, blending till smooth. Pour mixture into baked crust. Bake cheesecake at 350° till knife inserted just off-center comes out clean, 35 to 40 minutes. Top with reserved baked crumbs. Chill at least 4 hours. If desired, garnish with blanched whole almonds that have been dipped in melted unsweetened or semisweet chocolate. Makes 12 to 16 servings.

A special occasion calls for the French classic, sponge cake—Gateau Almond with Buttercream. An elegant apricot-brandy filling and smooth coffee-flavored frosting complement the delicate fine-textured cake.

Chocolate-Mint Torte

This elegant dessert is shown on page 6—

> **4 eggs**
> **1 package 2-layer-size German chocolate cake mix**
> **1 4¼- or 4½-ounce package instant chocolate pudding mix**
> **⅓ cup cooking oil**
> **½ cup mint-flavored semisweet chocolate pieces (½ of a 6-ounce package)**
> **2 teaspoons cooking oil**
> **2 2- or 2⅛-ounce packages dessert topping mix**

In large mixer bowl beat eggs till thick and lemon-colored. Blend in cake mix, dry pudding mix, the ⅓ cup cooking oil, and 1 cup water. Beat 4 minutes at medium speed of electric mixer. Pour into 2 greased and floured 9x1½-inch round baking pans. Bake at 350° till cakes test done, about 30 minutes. Cool 10 minutes before removing from pans. Cool thoroughly. Split each cake layer in half crosswise for a total of 4 layers. Melt together mint-flavored chocolate pieces and the 2 teaspoons cooking oil; stir well to combine. Prepare dessert topping mix according to package directions; set aside 2 cups whipped topping. Place one cake layer on serving plate; spread with *half the remaining* whipped topping. Place a second layer of cake atop; spread with *half* the melted chocolate. Repeat layers. (Top layer should have chocolate.) Frost sides of cake with the 2 cups reserved topping. Chill 2 to 3 hours. To serve, let stand at room temperature 15 minutes before cutting. Serves 16.

Fix a Frozen Dessert

Vanilla Ice Cream Dessert

Just as pretty in individual molds—

> **Shortening**
> ⅓ **cup chopped almonds, toasted**
>
> • • •
>
> 1 **cup crumbled soft coconut**
> **macaroons (6 cookies)**
> ¼ **cup orange-flavored liqueur**
> 1 **quart vanilla ice cream, softened**
> ½ **cup whipping cream**
> **Peach Sauce**

Generously coat inside of 5-cup mold with shortening; press in chopped almonds. Place in freezer. Meanwhile, stir crumbled macaroon cookies and orange-flavored liqueur into softened vanilla ice cream. Whip cream just till soft peaks form. Fold into ice cream mixture. Carefully spoon into prepared mold. Freeze. Unmold. Serve with warm Peach Sauce.

Peach Sauce: Combine 1 tablespoon orange-flavored liqueur and 1 tablespoon cornstarch; stir in two 10-ounce packages frozen peaches, thawed. Cook and stir till bubbly.

Dazzle the guests at your next party with a glamorous dessert that waits in the freezer till you're ready to serve. Spoon the warm orange liqueur and peach sauce over Vanilla Ice Cream Dessert *as the evening's finale.*

Daiquiri Dessert

Wedges of raspberry and lime sherbet are delicately accented with rum in the dessert topping —

> 3 2- or 2⅛-ounce packages
> dessert topping mix
> 1 cup milk
> ⅓ cup light rum
> 1 pint raspberry sherbet
> ½ cup flaked coconut
> 1 pint lime sherbet

Prepare topping mixes according to package directions, *except* omit the vanilla and use the milk and rum instead of liquid called for on package. Pipe through large star tip of pastry tube onto serving plate to form a ring 8 inches in diameter and 2 to 3 inches tall. Freeze firm.

Stir raspberry sherbet to soften; stir in *half* the coconut. Spoon into shell; freeze. Stir lime sherbet to soften; stir in remaining coconut and spoon atop pink layer. Cover and freeze till firm. If desired, trim with lime slices to serve. Makes 8 servings.

Butterscotch Bombe

Warm praline sauce adds extra goodness —

> 1 cup finely crushed gingersnaps
> 3 tablespoons butter or margarine,
> melted
> 1 quart vanilla ice cream
> 2 1⅛-ounce chocolate-coated
> English toffee bars, crushed
> Mellow Praline Sauce

Combine gingersnap crumbs and butter or margarine. Press crumb mixture firmly into 5-cup mold; freeze. Stir ice cream to soften; blend in the crushed candy. Spoon into crumb-lined mold; smooth top. Cover and freeze firm. To serve, remove cover and invert mold on chilled plate. Rub mold with warm, damp towel to loosen; remove mold. Cut into wedges; pass warm Mellow Praline Sauce. Serves 10.

Mellow Praline Sauce: In small saucepan combine ½ cup packed brown sugar, ½ cup light cream, and ¼ cup butter or margarine. Bring to boiling, stirring constantly. Remove from heat; stir in ¼ cup toasted chopped almonds and 1 teaspoon vanilla. Makes 1½ cups.

Frozen dessert tip

To unmold frozen desserts, invert the mold on a chilled serving plate. Rub mold with a hot, damp cloth just till loosened. Carefully lift off the mold.

Peach-Fig Bombe

A special dessert with only 102 calories a serving —

> 1 16-ounce can peach slices (juice
> pack)
> 1 envelope unflavored gelatin
> 1 tablespoon sugar
> ½ teaspoon vanilla
> Few drops yellow food coloring
> • • •
> 1 envelope from a 2½-ounce package
> low-calorie dessert topping mix
> 2 beaten eggs
> ½ cup reconstituted nonfat dry milk
> 1 teaspoon sugar
> ¼ teaspoon almond extract
> ¼ teaspoon vanilla
> 2 fig bars, crumbled

DIET DESSERT • DIET DESSERT

Pour undrained peaches into blender container; blend till puréed. In saucepan combine gelatin and 1 tablespoon sugar. Add peaches. Heat and stir over low heat just till mixture begins to boil. Remove from heat. Add ½ teaspoon vanilla. Tint with food coloring. Cool. Pour into freezer tray; freeze firm.

Prepare topping mix according to package directions. Break peach mixture into chunks; place in chilled bowl. Beat smooth with electric mixer. Fold in *half* of the whipped topping. Turn mixture into chilled 4-cup metal bombe mold. Freeze firm.

In small saucepan combine eggs, milk, and 1 teaspoon sugar. Cook and stir over low heat till mixture coats metal spoon. Remove from heat; stir in extract and ¼ teaspoon vanilla. Cool. Fold into remaining whipped topping; stir in crumbled fig bars. Pour atop peach layer. Cover with foil. Freeze firm. To serve, remove foil and unmold. Let stand 10 to 15 minutes before serving. Serves 8.

Dessert Treasury

Steaming fruit pies, cakes, fruit desserts, puddings, and cookies—all are featured in this section. This dessert cornucopia includes Cranberry Meringue Pie, Saucy Pomegranate-Floating Island, Fresh Tangerine Sherbet, Cheesecake Surprise, Cheddar-Topped Poached Apples, and Brandied Kumquats. (See index for page numbers.)

Cakes

Red Devil's Food Cake

Light and luscious Sea Foam Frosting covers and fills the rich chocolate cake—

 1 cup sugar
 ½ cup shortening
 3 egg yolks
 1 teaspoon vanilla
 • • •
 2½ cups sifted cake flour
 ½ cup unsweetened cocoa powder
 1½ teaspoons baking soda
 1 teaspoon salt
 1⅓ cups cold water
 3 egg whites
 ¾ cup sugar
 Sea Foam Frosting
 1 1-ounce square unsweetened
 chocolate
 ½ teaspoon shortening

In bowl cream together the 1 cup sugar and ½ cup shortening till light. Add egg yolks, one at a time, and vanilla, beating well after each addition. Sift together cake flour, cocoa powder, baking soda, and salt; add to creamed mixture in bowl alternately with cold water, beating well after each addition.

Beat egg whites to soft peaks; gradually add the ¾ cup sugar, beating to stiff peaks. Fold into batter; blend well. Turn mixture into 2 greased and lightly floured 8x1½-inch round baking pans. Bake at 350° till cake tests done, 35 to 40 minutes. Fill and frost with Sea Foam Frosting. Melt unsweetened chocolate with ½ teaspoon shortening; drizzle around edge of frosted cake.

Sea Foam Frosting: In top of double boiler combine 2 egg whites, 1½ cups packed brown sugar, ⅓ cup cold water, 2 teaspoons light corn syrup *or* ¼ teaspoon cream of tartar, and dash salt. Beat ½ minute at low speed of electric mixer. Place over hot, not boiling water. (Upper pan should not touch water.) Cook, beating constantly, till stiff peaks form, about 7 minutes *(do not overcook)*. Remove from water. Beat in 1 teaspoon vanilla.

Chocolate Cheesecake Torte

This dreamy chocolate cake with cheesecake filling is pictured opposite the contents page—

 1 package 2-layer-size German
 chocolate cake mix
 1 11-ounce can mandarin orange
 sections
 1 envelope unflavored gelatin
 • • •
 1 8-ounce package cream cheese,
 softened
 1 cup sugar
 2 egg yolks
 ½ teaspoon grated lemon peel
 1 tablespoon lemon juice
 2 egg whites
 ½ cup whipping cream
 Powdered sugar

Prepare cake mix according to package directions. Pour cake batter into 2 greased and floured 9x1½-inch round baking pans. Bake at 350° till cakes test done, 25 to 30 minutes. Cool 10 minutes in pan. Remove from pans; cool cakes thoroughly on wire racks.

Drain mandarin orange sections, reserving ¼ cup syrup. Dice orange sections; set aside. Soften unflavored gelatin in reserved mandarin orange syrup. Place over hot water and stir to dissolve. Cool slightly.

Beat together cream cheese and sugar. Beat in egg yolks, peel, and juice. Stir in cooled gelatin. Beat egg whites till stiff; whip cream. Fold egg whites and whipped cream into gelatin mixture with oranges. Turn into 8x1½-inch round baking pan. Chill till set. Unmold onto bottom cake layer. Cover with second cake layer. Sift powdered sugar over top.

A classic man-pleasing cake

Cut big slices of light and tender Red Devil's Food → *Cake with sweet* Sea Foam Frosting *and serve to a special man; be ready for second helpings.*

Cake-making pointers

• To substitute all-purpose flour for cake flour, use the following formula: 1 cup minus 2 tablespoons sifted all-purpose flour equals 1 cup sifted cake flour.
• When a recipe calls for shortening, *do not* substitute butter, margarine, lard, or cooking oil. However, you can substitute margarine for butter.
• Eggs separate more readily when they are cold. However, egg whites whip up better if they are at room temperature.
• When beating egg whites, make sure the bowl and beater are completely clean. Any trace of fat or egg yolk will prevent the egg whites from reaching full volume.
• Allow melted chocolate to cool slightly before blending it into creamed mixture.
• When adding dry ingredients alternately with liquid, begin and end with dry ingredients. Be sure to beat the mixture till smooth after each addition.
• Preheat oven to the correct temperature before mixing the cake.
• For shortening-type cakes, grease and lightly flour bottoms of pans, or line bottoms with waxed or baking pan liner paper. Push batter to sides of pan. Tap pan lightly to remove air bubbles.
• Place cake pans as near the center of the oven as possible. Pans should not touch each other or oven sides. If necessary, stagger pans on two shelves; never place pans directly under each other.
• Test a cake for doneness in one or more of the following ways: cake is shrunk slightly from sides of pan, cake springs back when lightly pressed, or a wooden pick inserted in center comes out clean.
• Cool shortening layer cakes in pan 10 minutes; loaf cakes, 15 minutes. Loosen edges. Place inverted rack on cake; turn all over. Lift off pan. Put second rack on cake. Turn cake so top is up. Invert angel and sponge cakes in pan to cool.
• To split a cake layer, place wooden picks around sides of cake for a guide. Cut cake with a sharp, thin-bladed knife.

Hot Milk Sponge Cake

Beat 2 eggs till thick and lemon-colored. Slowly add 1 cup sugar and beat at medium speed of electric mixer for 4 to 5 minutes. Stir together 1 cup all-purpose flour, 1 teaspoon baking powder, and ¼ teaspoon salt.

Heat ½ cup milk and 1 tablespoon butter till butter melts; keep hot. Add dry ingredients to egg mixture; stir just till blended. Stir in hot milk mixture; blend well. Pour batter into greased 9x9x2-inch baking pan. Bake at 350° for 20 to 25 minutes. (Or fill greased muffin pans half full with batter. Bake at 375° about 20 minutes.) Frost with Broiled Frosting (see recipe, page 34).

Orange-Strawberry Cake

Delicate orange cake filled with strawberries—

  1¼ cups all-purpose flour
  ⅓ cup sugar
  6 egg yolks
  1 tablespoon grated orange peel
  ½ cup orange juice
  ⅔ cup sugar
  ¼ teaspoon salt
  6 egg whites
  1 teaspoon cream of tartar
  ½ cup sugar
  1½ cups whipping cream
  2 cups fresh strawberries, sliced and sweetened lightly

Combine flour and ⅓ cup sugar; set aside. Beat egg yolks till thick and lemon-colored, about 5 minutes. Add orange peel and juice; beat till very thick. Gradually add ⅔ cup sugar and salt, beating constantly. Sift flour mixture over yolk mixture, a little at a time, folding carefully just till blended.

Wash beaters. Beat egg whites and cream of tartar till soft peaks form. Gradually add ½ cup sugar, beating to stiff peaks. Fold yolk mixture into whites. Turn into *ungreased* 10-inch tube pan; bake at 325° till cake tests done, 55 minutes. Invert cake in pan to cool.

Split cake into 3 layers. Whip cream. Stack cake layers, topping each with one-third of the whipped cream and sliced strawberries. Trim top with whole berries, if desired.

Feather Sponge Cake

  6 egg yolks
1½ cups sugar
  ½ teaspoon vanilla
  ½ teaspoon orange or lemon extract
1½ cups sifted cake flour
  ¼ teaspoon salt
  6 egg whites
  ¾ teaspoon cream of tartar

Beat egg yolks till thick and lemon-colored. Add ½ cup cold water; continue beating till very thick, about 5 minutes in all. Gradually beat in sugar, vanilla, and extract.

Sift flour with salt; fold into egg yolk mixture a little at a time. Beat egg whites with cream of tartar till stiff peaks form. Fold into first mixture, turning bowl gradually. Bake in *ungreased* 10-inch tube pan at 325° about 1 hour. Invert in pan to cool.

Marble Chiffon Cake

Sift together 2½ cups sifted cake flour, 1½ cups sugar, 3 teaspoons baking powder, and 1 teaspoon salt. Make a well in the center of dry ingredients, and add in this order: ½ cup cooking oil; 7 egg yolks; ¾ cup cold water; and 1 teaspoon vanilla. Beat till satin smooth.

In a large bowl beat 7 egg whites with ½ teaspoon cream of tartar till very stiff peaks form. Pour egg yolk batter in thin stream over entire surface of egg whites, gently folding to blend. Remove one-third of the batter to a separate bowl. Blend together ¼ cup boiling water, 2 tablespoons sugar, and two 1-ounce envelopes no-melt unsweetened chocolate-flavored product. Gently fold chocolate mixture into the one-third portion of batter.

Spoon *half* of the light batter into an *un-greased* 10-inch tube pan; top with *half* of the chocolate batter. Repeat layers with remaining batter. With a narrow spatula, swirl gently through batters to form marbled pattern. Bake at 325° for 55 minutes; raise oven temperature to 350° and bake 10 minutes longer. (Cake is done if it springs back when you touch the surface lightly.) Invert cake in pan; cool thoroughly before removing from pan. Frost with a favorite chocolate frosting, if desired.

Special Sponge Cake

This cake has only 82 calories per serving when served plain. Also try topping it with slightly sweetened fruit, but add the extra calories—

  1 cup sifted cake flour
1¼ cups sifted powdered sugar
  5 egg yolks
  5 egg whites
  1 teaspoon vanilla
  ½ teaspoon cream of tartar
  ½ teaspoon almond extract

Combine flour and ½ cup of the powdered sugar; set aside. In large mixer bowl beat egg yolks with electric mixer till thick and lemon-colored. Gradually add remaining sugar and ½ teaspoon salt, beating constantly. Wash beaters; beat egg whites with vanilla, cream of tartar, and almond extract till soft peaks form. Gently fold yolk mixture into whites. Sift flour mixture over batter, *one-third* at a time; gently fold in. Bake in *ungreased* 9-inch tube pan at 325° for 55 minutes. Invert cake in pan; cool thoroughly. Makes 16 servings.

Applesauce Cake Roll

  3 eggs
  ¾ cup granulated sugar
  1 8-ounce can applesauce
  1 cup all-purpose flour
  ½ teaspoon baking powder
  ½ teaspoon baking soda
  ½ teaspoon ground cinnamon
  ¼ teaspoon ground cloves
    Powdered sugar
  1 cup whipping cream
  ⅓ cup chopped walnuts

Beat eggs till thick; gradually add granulated sugar, beating well. Add ½ cup applesauce. Stir together next 5 ingredients and ¼ teaspoon salt. Fold into egg mixture. Spread in greased and floured 15x10x1-inch jelly roll pan. Bake at 350° for 15 to 20 minutes. Immediately turn out onto towel sprinkled with powdered sugar. Roll up. Let cool on rack. Whip cream to soft peaks. Fold in remaining applesauce and nuts. Unroll cake; spread applesauce mixture over. Roll up; chill.

Orange Rum-Yum Cake

This delicious cake contains 89 calories a serving—

1 9-inch sponge cake
2 tablespoons shredded orange peel
1 cup orange juice
2 tablespoons sugar
1 teaspoon rum flavoring

Using fork, punch holes in top of cake at 1-inch intervals. Combine orange peel, juice, and sugar; bring to a boil. Remove from heat; stir in flavoring. Spoon evenly over cake, *a small amount at a time,* allowing cake to absorb all syrup. Chill. Makes 16 servings.

Vanilla-Sour Cream Cake

Flavored with Vanilla Sugar that ages two weeks—

1 cup Vanilla Sugar
6 tablespoons butter or margarine
1 teaspoon vanilla
1¾ cups sifted cake flour
1½ teaspoons baking powder
1 teaspoon salt
½ teaspoon baking soda
1 cup dairy sour cream
4 stiffly beaten egg whites
Fluffy White Frosting (see recipe, page 34)
Tinted coconut

Prepare Vanilla Sugar. Cream butter and Vanilla Sugar; add vanilla. Sift together dry ingredients; add to creamed mixture alternately with sour cream, beating just till mixed. Fold in egg whites. Pour into 2 greased and floured 8x1½-inch round baking pans. Bake at 350° for 30 to 35 minutes. Fill and frost with Fluffy White Frosting; sprinkle with coconut.

Vanilla Sugar: Split 1 or 2 vanilla beans in half; place in canister with 3 to 5 pounds sugar. Let age at least two weeks.

The anytime dessert

← *Serve elegant* Vanilla-Sour Cream Cake *at the first sign of spring—or anytime.* Vanilla Sugar, *a mixture of aged vanilla beans and sugar, gives flavor.*

Orange Cream Cake

2½ cups sifted cake flour
1⅔ cups sugar
3½ teaspoons baking powder
1 teaspoon salt
2 teaspoons grated orange peel
¾ cup orange juice
⅔ cup shortening
3 eggs
¼ teaspoon almond extract
Orange Cream Frosting

In bowl sift cake flour, sugar, baking powder, and salt; add peel, juice, and shortening. Beat 2 minutes at medium speed of electric mixer. Add eggs, almond extract, and ⅓ cup water; beat 2 minutes more. Pour into greased and floured 13x9x2-inch baking pan. Bake at 350° for 40 to 45 minutes. Cool in pan. Frost with Orange Cream Frosting.

Orange Cream Frosting: Combine 3 cups sifted powdered sugar, ⅓ cup shortening, ½ teaspoon shredded orange peel, ¼ cup *hot* orange juice, 1 teaspoon lemon juice, and dash salt. If desired, add a few drops yellow food coloring. Beat at high speed of electric mixer till smooth. Add more powdered sugar, if needed, to make of spreading consistency.

Pears Helene Cake

Grease and flour one 9x1½-inch round baking pan. In second 9x1½-inch round baking pan, melt ½ cup butter or margarine. Sprinkle ½ cup packed brown sugar over melted butter.

Use 4 pear halves and ¼ cup syrup from one 16-ounce can pear halves; slice each pear halve lengthwise into thirds. Arrange with 16 pecan halves and 16 maraschino cherries in butter-brown sugar mixture.

Add water to reserved pear syrup to equal liquid called for on one package 2-layer-size yellow cake mix. Prepare cake mix according to directions, *except* use the pear liquid; divide batter between prepared pans. Bake according to package directions. Invert pan with pears on wire rack; cool layers about 10 minutes before removing pans. With one can ready-to-spread chocolate frosting, frost plain layer; cover with fruited layer. Frost sides.

Honey-Pecan Cake

Combine 1 tablespoon vinegar and enough milk to make 1 cup; set aside. In mixer bowl stir 1 cup cooking oil into 1½ cups sugar; add 3 eggs and 1 teaspoon vanilla. Beat 1 minute at medium speed of electric mixer. Stir together thoroughly 2 cups all-purpose flour, 3 teaspoons baking powder, 1 teaspoon ground cinnamon, ½ teaspoon baking soda, and ¼ teaspoon ground cloves. Add to oil-egg mixture alternately with milk mixture. Beat 1 minute more. Stir in ½ cup chopped pecans. Pour into *greased* 10-inch fluted tube pan. Bake at 350° for 40 minutes. Let stand 10 minutes. Remove from pan. Prick holes in hot cake with fork; drizzle cake with hot Honey Syrup.

Honey Syrup: Boil ¼ cup honey, 1 tablespoon water, and 1 tablespoon lemon juice.

Marble Pound Cake

> 1¼ cups sugar
> ¾ cup butter or margarine, softened
> ½ cup milk
> 1 teaspoon grated lemon peel
> 1 tablespoon lemon juice
> 2¼ cups sifted cake flour
> 1 teaspoon baking powder
> 3 eggs
> 2 tablespoons boiling water
> 1 tablespoon sugar
> 1 1-ounce square unsweetened
>   chocolate, melted and cooled

Gradually beat 1¼ cups sugar into butter; cream till light and fluffy, 8 to 10 minutes at medium speed of electric mixer. Beat in milk, peel, and juice. Sift together flour, baking powder, and 1¼ teaspoons salt. Add to creamed mixture; mix on low speed till smooth, about 2 minutes. Add eggs, one at a time, beating 1 minute after each. Beat 1 minute more, scraping sides of bowl frequently. Combine remaining ingredients; stir into *half* the batter. In greased 9x5x3-inch loaf pan, alternate spoonfuls of light and dark batters. With narrow spatula gently stir through batter to marble. Bake at 300° about 1 hour and 20 minutes. Cool 10 minutes; remove from pan. Cool. Sift powdered sugar atop, if desired.

Spicy Angel Cake

This cake has 85 calories per serving; topping is 15 calories for each tablespoon—

> 1 package two-step angel cake mix
> 1 teaspoon ground cinnamon
> ½ teaspoon ground nutmeg
> ¼ teaspoon ground ginger
> ¼ teaspoon ground cloves
> Maple Fluff Topping

In mixing bowl sift together dry flour mixture from cake mix and spices. Prepare and bake cake according to package directions. Invert; cool thoroughly in pan. Remove from pan; cut into eighteen 1-inch slices. Serve with Maple Fluff Topping. Makes 18 servings.

Maple Fluff Topping: Gently stir ¼ teaspoon maple flavoring into 1 cup frozen whipped dessert topping, thawed.

Strawberry Shortcake

> 4 cups all-purpose flour
> ¼ cup sugar
> 6 teaspoons baking powder
> 1 cup butter or margarine
> 2 beaten eggs
> 1⅓ cups light cream
>   Butter or margarine
> 1 cup whipping cream, whipped
> 3 to 4 cups sliced strawberries,
>   sweetened

Stir together dry ingredients and 1 teaspoon salt; cut in 1 cup butter till mixture resembles coarse crumbs. Combine eggs and cream; add to dry ingredients, stirring to moisten. Spread in 2 greased 8x1½-inch round baking pans; build up edges. Bake at 450° for 15 to 18 minutes. Remove from pans; cool on racks 5 minutes. Spread one layer with butter. Spoon berries and cream between layers and on top.

Dessert lovers' traditional favorite

No one can resist the juicy goodness of strawberries →
tucked inside flaky shortcake. Sweetened whipped cream complements Strawberry Shortcake.

Pumpkin-Spice Torte

In large mixer bowl combine one package 2-layer-size spice cake mix, one 16-ounce can pumpkin, 2 eggs, ⅓ cup water, and 2 teaspoons baking soda. Beat according to package directions. Pour into 2 greased and lightly floured 9x1½-inch round baking pans. Bake at 350° for 25 to 30 minutes. Let cool 10 minutes. Remove from pans; cool completely.

Meanwhile, prepare one 4½- or 5-ounce package *regular* vanilla pudding mix according to package directions, *except use 2¼ cups milk*. Cool; stir in ½ cup chopped walnuts. Split each cake layer in half crosswise. Put the layers together with pudding mixture.

Whip two 2-ounce packages dessert topping mix according to package directions. Spread over sides and top of cake. Drizzle Caramel Glaze down sides and edge of cake.

Caramel Glaze: Melt one 1⅜-ounce box round milk chocolate-covered caramels and 1 tablespoon butter in 2 tablespoons milk; stir constantly. Beat in ½ cup sifted powdered sugar. Cool. Add extra milk, if needed, to make pourable consistency.

Orange-Date Coffee Cake

>   2 cups all-purpose flour
>   ½ cup granulated sugar
>   3 teaspoons baking powder
>   1 slightly beaten egg
>   ½ cup milk
>   ½ cup cooking oil
>   ½ cup snipped dates
>   2 teaspoons grated orange peel
>   ½ cup orange juice
>   ½ cup packed brown sugar
>   2 tablespoons butter, softened
>   1 teaspoon ground cinnamon
>   ½ cup chopped walnuts

Stir together first 3 ingredients and ½ teaspoon salt. Combine egg, milk, and oil; add all at once to dry ingredients. Stir till mixed. Combine dates, peel, and juice; stir into batter just till blended. Spread evenly in greased 11x7½ x1½-inch baking pan. Mix remaining ingredients. Sprinkle over batter. Bake at 375° for 25 to 30 minutes. Serve warm.

Best-Ever Fruitcake

In large mixing bowl stir together thoroughly 3 cups all-purpose flour, 2 teaspoons baking powder, 2 teaspoons ground cinnamon, 1 teaspoon salt, ½ teaspoon ground nutmeg, ½ teaspoon ground allspice, and ½ teaspoon ground cloves. Add one 16-ounce package mixed candied fruits and peels (2½ cups); one 15-ounce package raisins (3 cups); one 8-ounce package whole candied cherries (1½ cups); one 8-ounce package pitted dates, snipped; 1 cup slivered almonds; 1 cup pecan halves; and ½ cup candied pineapple, chopped. Mix till fruits and nuts are well coated.

Melt ¾ cup butter or margarine; cool. Beat 4 eggs till foamy. Gradually add 1¾ cups packed brown sugar, beating till well combined. Blend in 1 cup orange juice, ¼ cup light molasses, and the cooled, melted butter. Add to fruit mixture; stir till well combined.

Turn batter into 2 greased and waxed paper-lined 8x4x2½-inch loaf pans, filling each ¾ full. Bake at 300° till done, 1¾ to 2 hours. Cool thoroughly before removing from pans.

Chocolate Cheesecake

>   1 10¾- or 11-ounce package
>   cheesecake mix
>   ¼ cup butter or margarine, melted
>   3 tablespoons sugar
>   1½ cups cold milk
>   1 tablespoon sugar
>   1 1-ounce envelope no-melt unsweet-
>   ened chocolate-flavored product
>   ½ cup dairy sour cream
>   Chocolate curls

Combine crumbs from the cheesecake mix, melted butter or margarine, and 3 tablespoons sugar. Press crumb mixture onto bottom and 1 inch up sides of 7½-inch springform pan. Chill.

In mixer bowl combine milk, the filling from the cheesecake mix, and 1 tablespoon sugar. Beat at low speed of electric mixer till blended; beat at medium speed for 3 minutes. Add chocolate; beat at low speed 1 minute more. Pour into crust; spread sour cream over top. Chill at least 1 hour. Garnish with chocolate curls. Makes 6 to 8 servings.

Cheesecake Surprise

This fruit-filled cake is pictured on page 23 —

⅔ **cup all-purpose flour**
2 **tablespoons granulated sugar**
6 **tablespoons butter or margarine**
1 **beaten egg yolk**
2 **8-ounce packages cream cheese**
⅔ **cup granulated sugar**
1 **tablespoon all-purpose flour**
1 **teaspoon vanilla**
4 **eggs**
1 **egg white**
2 **cups diced, peeled, fresh pears**
½ **cup fudge topping**
1 **cup dairy sour cream**
⅓ **cup powdered sugar**
½ **teaspoon vanilla**

Stir together first 2 ingredients and ¼ teaspoon salt. Cut in butter till crumbly; stir in egg yolk. Press evenly onto bottom of 9-inch springform pan. Bake at 350° for 18 minutes; cool. Reduce oven temperature to 325°.

In large mixer bowl beat together cream cheese, ⅔ cup granulated sugar, and 1 tablespoon flour till creamy. Add 1 teaspoon vanilla. Beat in the eggs and egg white till well blended. Stir in diced pears. Turn into cooled crust. Bake at 325° till knife inserted just off-center comes out clean, about 1 hour and 10 minutes. Carefully spread fudge topping over baked filling. Combine remaining ingredients; mix well. Swirl sour cream mixture into chocolate. Return to oven; bake 5 minutes more. Chill several hours or overnight. Garnish with fresh pear slices, if desired.

Tuck company special Chocolate Cheesecake *in refrigerator till serving time. The velvety chocolate filling is made easily with a convenience food; the smooth topper is dairy sour cream dotted with chocolate curls.*

Frostings and Toppings

Frosting tips

- Cool cake completely before frosting.
- Place three or four strips of waxed paper over edges of plate to keep plate clean while frosting cake. Carefully pull waxed paper strips out after frosting.
- Brush crumbs from cake. Position first layer top side *down* on plate. Spread with filling; place second layer top side *up*. Place tube cakes top side *down* to frost.
- Frost sides of cake first, then the top.
- Cut frosted cake with a sharp, thin-bladed knife dipped in warm water occasionally. Cut foam-type cakes with cake breaker or knife with serrated blade.

Seven-Minute Frosting

    2 unbeaten egg whites
 1½ cups sugar
    2 teaspoons light corn syrup
        or ¼ teaspoon cream of tartar
    1 teaspoon vanilla

In top of double boiler combine whites, sugar, corn syrup *or* cream of tartar, ⅓ cup cold water, and dash salt (don't place over boiling water). Beat ½ minute at low speed of electric mixer. Place over, but not touching boiling water. Cook, beating constantly, till stiff peaks form, *about* 7 minutes *(don't overcook)*. Remove from boiling water. (If desired, pour frosting into mixing bowl.) Add vanilla; beat till of spreading consistency, about 2 minutes. Frosts two 8- or 9-inch cake layers.

Chocolate Frosting

Prepare Seven-Minute Frosting. Fold in two 1-ounce squares unsweetened chocolate, melted and cooled, just before frosting cake.

Broiled Frosting

    ½ cup packed brown sugar
    6 tablespoons butter, melted
    ¼ cup light cream
    ½ teaspoon vanilla
    1 cup flaked coconut

Combine first 4 ingredients. Stir in coconut. Spread over baked one-layer cake in pan. Broil 4 to 5 inches from the heat till brown and bubbly, about 3 minutes. Serve warm or cold.

Fluffy White Frosting

In saucepan combine 1 cup sugar, ⅓ cup water, ¼ teaspoon cream of tartar, and dash salt. Bring to boiling, stirring till sugar dissolves. Very slowly add sugar syrup to 2 unbeaten egg whites in mixer bowl, beating constantly with electric mixer till stiff peaks form, about 7 minutes. Beat in 1 teaspoon vanilla. Frost tops and sides of two 8- or 9-inch cake layers or one 10-inch tube cake.

Butter Frosting

    6 tablespoons butter
    1 16-ounce package powdered sugar,
        sifted (about 4¾ cups)
       Light cream (about ¼ cup)
 1½ teaspoons vanilla

Cream butter; gradually add about *half* the sugar; mix well. Beat in *2 tablespoons* cream and vanilla. Gradually blend in remaining sugar. Add enough cream to make of spreading consistency. Frosts two 8- or 9-inch layers.

Confectioners' Icing

Add enough light cream to 2 cups sifted powdered sugar to make of spreading consistency. Add dash salt and 1 teaspoon vanilla.

Fudge Frosting

Smooth chocolate frosting spreads easily —

3 cups sugar
1 cup milk
3 tablespoons light corn syrup
2 1-ounce squares unsweetened
  chocolate
¼ teaspoon salt
¼ cup butter or margarine
1 teaspoon vanilla

Butter sides of heavy 3-quart saucepan. In it combine first 5 ingredients. Cook and stir over low heat till sugar dissolves and chocolate melts. Cook to soft-ball stage (234°) without stirring. Remove from heat; add butter and cool to warm (110°) without stirring. Add vanilla; beat till mixture is of spreading consistency. Frosts two 9-inch layers.

Chocolate Glaze

It hardens to a smooth, glossy finish —

1½ 1-ounce squares unsweetened
  chocolate
2 tablespoons butter or margarine
1½ cups sifted powdered sugar
1 teaspoon vanilla
3 tablespoons boiling water

Melt chocolate and butter or margarine over low heat, stirring constantly. Remove from heat. Stir in powdered sugar and vanilla until crumbly. Blend in boiling water. Add enough water (about 2 teaspoons), a teaspoon at a time, to form medium glaze of pouring consistency. Pour quickly over top of cake; spread glaze evenly over top and sides.

Lemon Butter Frosting

Fresh grated lemon peel gives tang —

Cream ¼ cup butter or margarine; gradually add 2 cups sifted powdered sugar, blending till smooth. Add 1 teaspoon grated lemon peel and 1 tablespoon lemon juice; beat till mixture is smooth. Stir in enough milk (1 to 2 teaspoons) to make the frosting of proper spreading consistency. Frosts 18 cupcakes.

Three-Way Cream Cheese Frosting

1 3-ounce package cream cheese,
  softened
1 tablespoon butter or
  margarine, softened
1 teaspoon shredded orange peel
  or 1 teaspoon vanilla or 1
  1-ounce square unsweetened
  chocolate, melted and cooled
2 cups sifted powdered sugar

Combine cream cheese, butter, and orange peel *or* vanilla *or* chocolate. Beat at low speed of electric mixer till light and fluffy. Gradually add sugar; continue beating till fluffy. If necessary, add more liquid (2 teaspoons milk *or* ½ teaspoon orange juice) to make of spreading consistency. Frosts a one-layer cake.

Caramel-Cream Cheese Frosting

7 vanilla caramels
1 tablespoon hot water
1 3-ounce package cream cheese,
  softened
2½ cups sifted powdered sugar
⅛ teaspoon salt

Combine caramels and hot water in 2-cup glass measuring cup or small heatproof glass dish. Place in small saucepan of gently boiling water. Heat and stir till caramels melt and sauce is smooth. Cool. Beat together softened cream cheese and sugar. Add cooled sauce and salt; mix well. Frosts a one-layer cake.

Lemon Delight Frosting

6 tablespoons butter or margarine,
  softened
1 16-ounce package powdered sugar,
  sifted
½ of a 6-ounce can frozen lemonade
  concentrate, thawed (⅓ cup)

In mixing bowl cream together butter or margarine and sifted powdered sugar. Gradually add lemonade concentrate. Beat till fluffy. Frosts one 13x9x2-inch cake.

Butter-Rum Sauce

1 cup packed brown sugar
3 tablespoons all-purpose flour
¼ teaspoon salt
½ cup water
1 6-ounce can evaporated milk
¼ cup light corn syrup
½ cup coarsely chopped salted
    mixed nuts
2 tablespoons butter or margarine
2 teaspoons rum flavoring

In heavy saucepan combine first 3 ingredients; stir in water. Stir in evaporated milk and syrup. Cook, stirring constantly, till thickened. Stir in remaining ingredients. Serve warm over ice cream or cake. Makes 2 cups.

Chocolate Velvet Sauce

In saucepan combine one 6-ounce package semisweet chocolate pieces and ⅔ cup light corn syrup; cook and stir over low heat till chocolate melts. Remove from heat; cool. Stir in one 6-ounce can evaporated milk. Serve warm or chilled over ice cream or cake. Store, covered, in refrigerator. Makes 1⅔ cups.

Custard Sauce

In heavy saucepan mix 4 beaten egg yolks, ¼ cup sugar, and dash salt. Gradually stir in 2 cups milk, scalded and slightly cooled. Cook and stir over low heat till mixture coats metal spoon. Remove from heat. Cool pan at once in cold water; stir a minute or two. Add 1 teaspoon vanilla. Chill. Serve over baked puddings, soufflés, or fruit. Makes 2 cups.

Hard Sauce

Thoroughly cream ½ cup butter with 2 cups sifted powdered sugar. Add 1 teaspoon vanilla. Spread in 8x8x2-inch pan; chill. Cut in squares. Serve with baked or steamed puddings.

Fluffy Hard Sauce: Stir 1 beaten egg yolk into creamed mixture above. Fold in 1 stiffly beaten egg white. Chill.

Orange Sauce

Enhance the flavor of pound cake slices or hot fruit dumplings with this delicate sauce —

¼ cup sugar
1 tablespoon cornstarch
1 cup orange juice
• • •
1 tablespoon butter or margarine
2 teaspoons lemon juice

In saucepan combine sugar and cornstarch. Stir in orange juice; cook, stirring constantly, till mixture thickens and bubbles. Remove from heat; stir in butter or margarine and lemon juice. Makes about 1 cup.

Peppermint Sauce

This easy-to-fix sauce starts with marshmallow creme and peppermint candy —

2 7- or 9-ounce jars marshmallow creme
½ cup finely crushed peppermint candy
⅓ cup milk
Red food coloring (optional)

In saucepan heat and stir marshmallow creme over low heat till softened. Blend in crushed candy and milk. Tint pink with food coloring, if desired. Stir before serving, adding more milk, if necessary, to make of desired consistency. Serve warm or cooled over ice cream. Makes about 2½ cups.

Raspberry Sauce

A crimson berry sauce that's delicious served over ice cream or cake —

2 10-ounce packages frozen red
    raspberries
¼ cup sugar
1 tablespoon cornstarch

Thaw and drain raspberries, reserving ½ cup syrup. In small bowl combine sugar and cornstarch. In small saucepan heat reserved syrup to boiling. Quickly stir into cornstarch mixture; return all to saucepan. Quickly cook and stir till mixture is thick and bubbly. Cool; stir in raspberries. Makes 1⅓ cups.

Whip up easy Blueberry Sauce to serve over tender cake slices; no one will miss frosting, and they'll enjoy the switch to this sweet berry sauce. Serve the pretty leftover fruit sauce over vanilla pudding another time.

Blueberry Sauce

Serve this refreshing sauce over slices of angel cake or lemon-flavored pound cake—

    1 9- or 10-ounce package frozen
        unsweetened blueberries
    1 cup sugar
    3 tablespoons cornstarch
    1 cup boiling water
            • • •
    3 tablespoons lemon juice

Thaw and drain frozen unsweetened blueberries. In small saucepan combine sugar and cornstarch; gradually stir in boiling water. Cook, stirring constantly, till mixture is thickened and bubbly; cook 2 minutes more. Remove from heat; stir in drained blueberries and lemon juice. Cool. Makes 3 cups sauce.

Ambrosia Sauce

    1 16-ounce can fruit cocktail
    2 tablespoons sugar
    2 teaspoons cornstarch
        Dash salt
    2 tablespoons water
    2 tablespoons frozen orange juice
        concentrate, thawed
    1 orange, peeled and diced
    ½ cup flaked coconut

Drain fruit cocktail, reserving 1 cup syrup. In saucepan combine sugar, cornstarch, and salt; blend in water. Add reserved syrup and orange juice concentrate. Cook and stir till mixture thickens and bubbles. Stir in fruit cocktail, diced orange, and coconut. Chill. Serve over vanilla ice cream. Makes 2½ cups.

Burgundy-Cherry Sauce

1 16-ounce can dark sweet
   cherries
2 tablespoons cornstarch
2 tablespoons sugar
¼ cup water
¼ cup red Burgundy

Drain cherries, reserving syrup. In small saucepan combine cornstarch and sugar. Gradually stir in reserved syrup and water. Cook and stir over medium heat till thick and bubbly. Stir in cherries; heat through. Remove from heat; stir in Burgundy. Serve warm over cake.

Flaming Ice Cream Sauce

½ cup sugar
1 cup orange juice
2 cups cubed, peeled fresh
   pineapple
2 bananas, sliced
⅓ cup light rum

Put sugar in large, heavy skillet. Heat and stir over low heat till sugar is melted. When mixture is golden, remove skillet from heat and slowly stir in orange juice. Heat and stir till caramelized sugar is dissolved. Simmer, uncovered, for 8 to 10 minutes. Gently stir in pineapple and banana; heat till mixture is warm. In small saucepan or ladle, heat rum; flame. Pour flaming rum over pineapple mixture. Serve immediately over vanilla ice cream or pineapple sherbet. Makes 8 to 10 servings.

Hot Fudge-Nut Sauce

1 6-ounce package semisweet
   chocolate pieces
1 cup milk
½ cup sugar
½ cup peanut butter

In small saucepan combine chocolate pieces, milk, and sugar. Bring to boiling, stirring constantly. Gradually stir chocolate mixture into peanut butter. Serve warm sauce atop ice cream or pound cake. Makes 2 cups.

Easy Butter-Rum Sauce

Before serving leftover sauce, thin with a little more milk and rum, then heat through —

¼ cup butter or margarine
2 tablespoons light corn syrup
1 package creamy white frosting
   mix (for 2-layer cake)
⅓ cup evaporated milk
   • • •
¼ cup rum
½ cup chopped pecans

In saucepan brown the butter; remove from heat. Blend in corn syrup and *about half* the frosting mix; add remaining mix and gradually stir in evaporated milk. Heat through, stirring constantly. Remove from heat; stir in rum and nuts. Serve over ice cream. Makes 2 cups.

Cool Dessert Topping

Creamy-smooth topping is 10 calories a tablespoon —

½ teaspoon unflavored
   gelatin
⅔ cup water
1 cup frozen whipped
   dessert topping, thawed

In small saucepan soften gelatin in water; stir over low heat till gelatin dissolves. Chill till partially set. Beat with electric mixer till doubled. Add topping; beat to soft peaks. Chill. Stir gently before serving with puddings or with fruit desserts. Makes 1⅔ cups.

Applesauce Topper

Serve big scoops of topper over fresh-from-the-oven gingerbread or spice cake —

1 8½-ounce can applesauce
3 tablespoons red cinnamon candies
4 or 5 drops red food coloring
1 quart vanilla ice cream, softened

In saucepan combine applesauce, cinnamon candies, and food coloring. Heat till candy is dissolved. Cool. Stir cooled applesauce mixture into softened ice cream. Freeze applesauce mixture at least 6 hours or overnight.

Lemon Filling

¾ cup sugar
2 tablespoons cornstarch
¾ cup cold water
2 slightly beaten egg yolks
1 teaspoon grated lemon peel
3 tablespoons lemon juice
1 tablespoon butter or margarine

In saucepan combine sugar, cornstarch, and dash salt; gradually stir in cold water. Stir in egg yolks, lemon peel, and juice. Cook and stir over medium heat till thickened and bubbly. Boil 1 minute; remove from heat. Stir in butter or margarine. Cool to room temperature without stirring. Makes 1⅓ cups.

Lime Filling

Prepare Lemon Filling, substituting 1 teaspoon grated lime peel and 3 tablespoons lime juice for lemon peel and lemon juice. Add 1 drop green food coloring with the butter.

Orange Filling

Prepare Lemon Filling, substituting ¾ cup orange juice for ¾ cup water and the 3 tablespoons lemon juice. Omit grated lemon peel.

Custard Filling

⅓ cup sugar
2 tablespoons all-purpose flour
1 tablespoon cornstarch
¼ teaspoon salt
1½ cups milk
1 egg
1 egg yolk
1 teaspoon vanilla

Combine first 4 ingredients. Gradually add milk; mix well. Cook and stir till thick and bubbly; cook 2 to 3 minutes more. Beat together egg and egg yolk. Stir a little of the hot mixture into egg; return to hot mixture. Cook and stir till bubbly. Stir in vanilla. Cover with waxed paper; cool. Makes about 1¾ cups.

Cream Filling

Delicate vanilla-flavored filling —

⅓ cup granulated sugar
3 tablespoons all-purpose flour
¼ teaspoon salt
1¼ cups milk
1 beaten egg
1 tablespoon butter
1 teaspoon vanilla

In saucepan combine sugar, all-purpose flour, and salt. Gradually add milk; mix well. Cook and stir over medium heat till mixture thickens and bubbles; cook and stir 2 minutes longer. Very gradually stir the hot mixture into the egg; return to saucepan. Cook and stir till mixture just boils. Stir in butter and vanilla; cover surface with waxed paper or clear plastic wrap. Cool. (Don't stir during cooling.) Makes 1½ cups.

Butterscotch Filling

Prepare Cream Filling, substituting ⅓ cup packed brown sugar for ⅓ cup granulated sugar. Increase butter to 2 tablespoons.

Chocolate Filling

Prepare Cream Filling, increasing granulated sugar to ½ cup. Add one 1-ounce square unsweetened chocolate, cut up, with milk.

Grasshopper Filling

Layer this minty filling between chocolate cake layers for an elegant dessert —

1 envelope unflavored gelatin
¼ cup cold water
⅓ cup white crème de cacao
½ cup green crème de menthe
2 cups whipping cream

Soften gelatin in cold water. Heat together crème de cacao and crème de menthe. Add softened gelatin; stir till gelatin is dissolved. Cool. Whip cream; fold in gelatin mixture. Refrigerate 15 minutes. Makes about 4 cups.

Pies

Upside-Down Berry Meringue Pie

Taste-tempting pie pictured on cover—

    3 egg whites
    ½ teaspoon vinegar
    ¼ teaspoon salt
    ½ cup sugar
    ½ teaspoon vanilla
    1 baked 9-inch pastry shell
    3 cups fresh strawberries
    ⅓ cup sugar
    2 tablespoons cornstarch
    ½ cup water
      Several drops red food coloring
    1 cup whipping cream

Beat egg whites with vinegar and salt till soft peaks form. Gradually add ½ cup sugar and vanilla, beating to stiff peaks. Spread on bottom and sides of baked pastry shell. Bake at 325° for 12 minutes; cool. Mash and sieve *2 cups* of the strawberries. In saucepan blend ⅓ cup sugar and cornstarch. Add water and mashed berries. Cook and stir till mixture thickens and bubbles. Cook 2 minutes. Tint with food coloring; cool slightly. Spread over meringue; chill till set. Whip cream; spread over all. Slice whole berries for top.

Cranberry Meringue Pie

Unusual fruit pie shown on page 22—

In saucepan cook 3 cups cranberries in 1½ cups water, stirring till cranberries pop. Add ¾ cup light raisins. Combine 1¾ cups granulated sugar and ¼ cup cornstarch; add to cranberry mixture. Cook and stir till mixture thickens and bubbles. Stir in ½ cup chopped walnuts and 2 tablespoons butter till butter melts. Spoon into one *baked* 9-inch pastry shell.

Beat 3 egg whites till soft peaks form. Gradually add 6 tablespoons packed brown sugar and continue beating till stiff peaks form. Spread meringue atop hot cranberry filling, sealing to edges of pastry. Bake at 350° till golden brown, 12 to 15 minutes.

Lemonade Meringue Pie

Tangy lemonade flavor comes from convenient frozen lemonade concentrate—

In saucepan combine 1 cup dairy sour cream and 3 slightly beaten egg yolks. Stir in one 4½- or 5-ounce package *regular* vanilla pudding mix, 1¼ cups milk, and ⅓ cup frozen lemonade concentrate, thawed. Cook and stir till mixture thickens and bubbles. Remove from heat; spoon into one *baked* 9-inch pastry shell.

Beat 3 egg whites, ½ teaspoon vanilla, and ¼ teaspoon cream of tartar till soft peaks form. Gradually add 6 tablespoons sugar, beating till stiff peaks form. Spread atop hot filling, sealing to edges of pastry. Bake at 350° for 12 to 15 minutes. Cool; chill before serving.

S'More Pie

You will remember this flavor combination from your childhood camping days—

Prepare Graham Cracker Crust (see recipe, page 51); bake and cool. Combine 2 cups milk and 2 egg yolks; gradually add to one 3- or 3¼-ounce package *regular* vanilla pudding mix in saucepan. Cook according to package directions. Cover surface with waxed paper; cool.

Place 1 cup tiny marshmallows over crust; top with three ¾-ounce milk chocolate candy bars, broken in pieces. Spoon cooled pudding evenly over chocolate pieces.

Beat 2 egg whites with ½ teaspoon vanilla and ¼ teaspoon cream of tartar till soft peaks form. Gradually add ¼ cup sugar, beating till stiff peaks form. Spread meringue atop pie, sealing to edges. Bake at 350° till golden, 12 to 15 minutes. Cool thoroughly.

Lemonade lovers delight

*Swirl meringue atop hot pie filling to minimize →
weeping. Frozen lemonade and vanilla pudding mix make Lemonade Meringue Pie easy to prepare.*

Garnish airy Choco-Mint Pie with several dollops of whipped topping sprinkled with crushed peppermint candy. This unusual chiffon pie gets its refreshing flavor from peppermint extract and unsweetened chocolate.

Choco-Mint Pie

Peppermint extract and candy give refreshing zing to delicate, whipped pie—

- ½ cup sugar
- 1 envelope unflavored gelatin
  Dash salt
- 1 cup milk
- 2 1-ounce squares unsweetened chocolate, cut up
- 3 slightly beaten egg yolks
- ¼ teaspoon peppermint extract
- 3 egg whites
- ¼ cup sugar
- 1 pint frozen whipped dessert topping, thawed
- 1 baked 9-inch pastry shell
  Crushed peppermint stick candy (optional)

In medium saucepan combine ½ cup sugar, unflavored gelatin, and salt. Add milk and unsweetened chocolate. Cook and stir over low heat till gelatin is dissolved and chocolate is melted. Remove from heat; stir a small amount of hot mixture into slightly beaten egg yolks. Return to saucepan; cook and stir till mixture thickens and bubbles. Remove from heat; stir in peppermint extract. Cool till chocolate mixture is partially set.

In small mixing bowl beat egg whites till soft peaks form; gradually add the ¼ cup sugar. Beat till stiff peaks form. Fold into partially set chocolate mixture. Fold in thawed frozen whipped dessert topping. Turn mixture into baked pastry shell. Chill till filling is set. Garnish top of pie with additional whipped dessert topping and crushed peppermint stick candy, if desired.

Layered Pumpkin Chiffon Pie

Gingersnap Crust (see recipe, page 51)
⅓ cup granulated sugar
1 envelope unflavored gelatin
½ teaspoon ground cinnamon
½ teaspoon ground allspice
¼ teaspoon ground ginger
¼ teaspoon ground nutmeg
½ cup milk
3 egg yolks
1 cup canned or mashed cooked
   pumpkin
   • • •
3 egg whites
¼ cup granulated sugar
1 cup whipping cream
¼ cup sifted powdered sugar
½ teaspoon vanilla
¼ teaspoon ground cinnamon

Prepare Gingersnap Crust; set aside to cool. In saucepan combine ⅓ cup granulated sugar, gelatin, cinnamon, allspice, ginger, nutmeg, and ½ teaspoon salt. Stir in milk, egg yolks, and pumpkin. Cook and stir over medium heat till mixture bubbles and gelatin dissolves. Remove from heat; chill till partially set. Beat egg whites till soft peaks form. Gradually add ¼ cup granulated sugar; beat till stiff peaks form. Fold into pumpkin mixture. Pile half the mixture into cooled crust; set remaining aside.

Combine remaining ingredients; refrigerate half the mixture. Whip remaining half; spread over pumpkin mixture. Top with remaining pumpkin; chill till firm. To serve, whip reserved whipping cream mixture; pass with pie.

Mince Chiffon Pie

Cream sherry adds a gourmet touch—

Dissolve one 3-ounce package lemon-flavored gelatin and ¼ cup sugar in 1 cup boiling water; stir in 1 cup prepared mincemeat, ¼ cup cream sherry, and a few drops yellow food coloring. Chill till partially set. Beat 3 egg whites to soft peaks. Gradually add ¼ cup sugar; beat to stiff peaks. Whip ½ cup whipping cream; fold with egg whites into gelatin. Chill till mixture mounds; spoon into one *baked* 9-inch pastry shell. Chill. Top with whipped cream.

Pineapple Chiffon Pie

Each wedge of this dreamy pie adds 135 calories to the calorie counter's diet—

Yogurt Pastry (see recipe, page 50)
½ of a 20-ounce can crushed
   pineapple (juice pack)
1 4-serving envelope low-calorie
   lemon-flavored gelatin
½ cup cold water
3 beaten egg yolks
   • • •
3 egg whites
1 teaspoon vanilla
¼ teaspoon cream of tartar

Prepare Yogurt Pastry; set aside to cool. Drain pineapple, reserving juice. Combine gelatin and dash salt; stir in pineapple juice and cold water. Stir over low heat till gelatin dissolves. Stir a moderate amount of hot mixture into egg yolks. Return to saucepan; cook 2 minutes more. Stir in the drained pineapple. Chill till partially set.

Beat egg whites, vanilla, and cream of tartar till stiff peaks form. Fold in gelatin mixture. Turn into cooled, baked Yogurt Pastry shell. Chill till firm. Makes 8 servings.

Custard Pie

Vary the good old-fashioned flavor of this favorite with flaked coconut—

4 slightly beaten eggs
½ cup sugar
½ teaspoon vanilla
¼ teaspoon salt
2½ cups milk, scalded
1 unbaked 9-inch pastry shell
   Ground nutmeg

Blend eggs, sugar, vanilla, and salt. Gradually stir in scalded milk. Place pastry-lined pie plate on oven rack; pour filling into measuring cup. Pour filling into pastry shell. Sprinkle with ground nutmeg.

Bake at 350° till knife inserted halfway between center and edge comes out clean, 35 to 40 minutes. Cool on rack; then chill.

Note: If desired, omit nutmeg; sprinkle ½ cup flaked coconut atop unbaked filling.

All-American Apple Pie tastes doubly great served with Homemade Vanilla Ice Cream (see recipe, page 90). This pie also teams well with thick slices of your favorite cheese. Serve it either way with big mugs of hot coffee.

Apple Pie

    6 to 8 tart apples, peeled, cored,
       and thinly sliced (6 cups)
  ¾ to 1 cup sugar
  2 tablespoons all-purpose flour
  ½ to 1 teaspoon ground cinnamon
    Dash ground nutmeg
    Pastry for 2-crust pie
    Butter or margarine
    Sugar

If apples lack tartness, sprinkle with 1 tablespoon lemon juice. Combine dry ingredients; mix with apples. Line pie plate with pastry. Fill with apple mixture; dot with butter. Adjust top crust, cutting slits for escape of steam. Seal; flute edges. Sprinkle with sugar. Bake at 400° about 50 minutes.

Johnny Appleseed Pie

  ⅓ cup sugar
  1 teaspoon ground cinnamon
  6 to 8 tart apples, peeled, cored,
      and thinly sliced (6 cups)
  1 unbaked 9-inch pastry shell
  ½ cup semisweet chocolate pieces
  1 cup packaged biscuit mix
  ¼ cup sugar
  ¼ cup butter or margarine

Combine ⅓ cup sugar and cinnamon; mix with apples. Turn into unbaked pastry shell. Top with chocolate pieces. In small bowl combine biscuit mix and ¼ cup sugar. Cut in butter or margarine till mixture resembles coarse crumbs. Sprinkle evenly over pie. Bake at 400° till apples are tender, about 45 minutes.

Pear-Strawberry Glazed Pie

> 1 29-ounce can pear halves
> 1 10-ounce package frozen
>   strawberries, thawed
>   • • •
> 1 baked 9-inch pastry shell
> 2 tablespoons cornstarch
> ¼ cup currant jelly

Drain pears and strawberries, reserving syrups. Slice pears; arrange in pastry shell with berries. Measure reserved strawberry syrup; add pear syrup to equal 1 cup liquid. Stir syrup mixture into cornstarch; add currant jelly. Cook and stir till mixture thickens and bubbles; spoon over fruit. Top with whipped cream and a few halved strawberries, if desired.

Rhubarb and Cherry Pie

> 1 pound rhubarb, cut in ½-inch
>   slices (about 4 cups)
> 1 16-ounce can pitted tart red
>   cherries, drained
> 1½ cups sugar
> ¼ cup quick-cooking tapioca
> 5 drops red food coloring
>   Pastry for lattice-top pie

In mixing bowl combine rhubarb, cherries, sugar, tapioca, and food coloring; let stand 15 minutes. Line 9-inch pie plate with pastry; pour in filling. Adjust lattice top; seal and flute edges. Bake at 400° for 40 to 50 minutes.

Lemon-Crusted Blueberry Pie

Special Lemon Pastry makes this one different—

Prepare Lemon Pastry (see recipe, page 51). In mixing bowl combine 4 cups blueberries, ¾ to 1 cup sugar, 3 tablespoons all-purpose flour, ½ teaspoon grated lemon peel, and dash salt. Line 9-inch pie plate with pastry; pour in filling. Drizzle with 1 to 2 teaspoons lemon juice and dot with 1 tablespoon butter or margarine. Adjust top crust, cutting slits for escape of steam; seal and flute edges. Bake at 400° for 35 to 40 minutes. Sprinkle top crust with additional sugar, if desired.

Strawberry Glaze Pie

Glamorous pie becomes picture-perfect when each bright strawberry is individually placed—

> 6 cups medium-size strawberries
> 1 cup water
> ¾ cup sugar
> 3 tablespoons cornstarch
>   Red food coloring
> 1 baked 9-inch pastry shell

Wash berries; remove hulls. Crush 1 cup of the smaller berries and cook with the water about 2 minutes; sieve. Blend sugar and cornstarch; stir in berry juice. Cook and stir over medium heat till glaze is thickened and clear. Stir in about 5 drops red food coloring.

Spread a small amount of strawberry glaze (about ¼ cup) on bottom and sides of baked pastry shell. Arrange *half* the whole strawberries, stem end down, in pastry shell. Spoon *half* the remaining glaze carefully over berries, being sure each is well coated. Arrange remaining strawberries, stem end down, on first layer; spoon on remaining glaze, coating each berry. Chill 3 to 4 hours. If desired, garnish top of pie with whipped cream and a few additional whole strawberries.

Cranberry-Peach Pie

Toasted almonds add a delightful crunch to this mouth-watering cranberry and peach pie—

> 1 29-ounce can peach slices
> 3 cups cranberries
> 1½ cups sugar
> 3 tablespoons cornstarch
>   • • •
> ¼ cup chopped almonds, toasted
>   Pastry for lattice-top pie

Drain peaches, reserving 1 cup syrup; cut up peaches and set aside. In medium saucepan combine cranberries and peach syrup; cook till skins pop. Combine sugar and cornstarch. Add to hot cranberries. Cook quickly, stirring constantly, till mixture thickens and bubbles. Remove from heat. Stir in peaches and almonds. Line 9-inch pie plate with pastry; pour in filling. Adjust lattice top; seal and crimp edges high. Bake at 400° for 35 to 40 minutes; cool.

Piemaking tips

- The equipment necessary to make pie-making easier includes a pastry blender, a rolling pin with stockinette, a pastry cloth, and a pastry wheel.
- Prevent overbrowning the pastry edge by protecting it with a foil collar during part of the baking. Fold a 2½-inch strip of foil around the rim, making sure the foil covers all the fluted edge.
- Spread meringue carefully to the edge of pastry all the way around to prevent meringue from shrinking. Swirl meringue atop hot pie filling to reduce weeping and also to minimize shrinkage.
- Dip a knife in water before cutting a meringue-topped pie to prevent sticking. (No need to wipe off water from knife.)
- For a nonstick crumb crust, wrap a hot, wet towel under bottom and around sides of the pie plate just before serving the pie. Hold towel against plate for a few minutes; this loosens crust so pieces of pie will slip out easily.
- Decorate pie tops with pastry cutouts. Use a small cookie cutter or hors d'oeuvre cutter, or make your own pattern. Arrange cutouts on pie before baking, or bake separately and place on baked pie.
- Brush unbaked crust of two-crust pies with water or melted butter, and then sprinkle lightly with sugar to give pie a glazed finish. Or brush the crust lightly with beaten egg or a light coating of milk before baking for the same effect.
- For perfect chiffon pies, follow recipe directions carefully. Remember that partially set gelatin has started to gel but is still pourable.
- Place pastry-lined pie plate on oven rack before pouring in liquidy pie filling to avoid messy spills.
- Store pies properly and safely. Refrigerate pies with fillings containing any eggs or dairy products. Refrigerate pies containing gelatin. If necessary, you can store fruit pies at room temperature for a short period of time.

Pineapple Dream Pie

Celebrate an island holiday with this succulent pineapple pie with coconut crust—

    Coconut Crust (see recipe, page 51)
1 **3¼-ounce package regular vanilla tapioca pudding mix**
1 **3-ounce package lemon-flavored gelatin**
1¼ **cups milk**
  ½ **of a 6-ounce can frozen pineapple juice concentrate, thawed**

       • • •

1 **2-ounce package dessert topping mix**
1 **8¼-ounce can crushed pineapple, well drained (¾ cup)**

Prepare Coconut Crust; set aside to cool. Combine pudding mix and gelatin; stir in milk. Cook and stir till bubbly; remove from heat. Stir in concentrate; chill till partially set. Prepare topping mix following package directions. Fold into pudding mixture with pineapple. Turn into crust; chill 6 hours.

Lime Dream Pie

This pretty green pie gets its mouth-watering lime flavor from frozen limeade concentrate—

    Chocolate Wafer Crust (see recipe, page 51)
1¼ **cups sugar**
  ½ **cup all-purpose flour**
  ¼ **teaspoon salt**
1¾ **cups water**
  ½ **cup frozen limeade concentrate, thawed**
1 **drop green food coloring**
3 **slightly beaten egg yolks**
3 **tablespoons butter or margarine**
  ½ **cup whipping cream**

Prepare Chocolate Wafer Crust; chill. Combine sugar, flour, and salt; stir in water. Add concentrate and food coloring. Cook and stir till bubbly; cook and stir 2 minutes more. Stir small amount hot mixture into yolks; return to hot mixture. Cook and stir till bubbly; stir in butter. Pour into crust; cool. Whip cream; spread on pie. Chill.

Banana-Rum Pie

>   Pecan Pastry (see recipe, page 51)
>   1 3- or 3¼-ounce package regular
>   vanilla pudding mix
>   1 envelope unflavored gelatin
>   2¼ cups milk
>   • • •
>   1 package fluffy white frosting mix
>   (for 2-layer cake)
>   1½ teaspoons rum flavoring
>   Dash ground nutmeg
>   3 bananas
>   1 1-ounce square semisweet chocolate
>   1 tablespoon butter or margarine

Prepare Pecan Pastry; set aside. In saucepan combine pudding mix and gelatin. Cook according to pudding package directions, using the 2¼ cups milk. Remove from heat; cover surface with waxed paper and set aside.

Prepare frosting mix according to package directions. Stir in rum flavoring, nutmeg, and dash salt. Fold hot pudding into frosting. Slice *one* banana into pastry shell; cover with *half* the pudding mixture. Repeat with second banana and remaining pudding. Chill 3 to 4 hours. Diagonally slice remaining banana; arrange on pie. Melt together chocolate and butter; drizzle over banana.

Black Forest Cherry Pie

In saucepan combine ⅔ cup sugar, 3 table-spoons cornstarch, and ¼ teaspoon salt; gradually stir in 2 cups milk. Cook and stir till thick and bubbly; cook 2 minutes more. Stir small amount hot mixture into 2 slightly beaten eggs. Return to hot mixture; cook 2 minutes more. Remove from heat; stir in 2 tablespoons butter and 1 teaspoon vanilla.

Melt two 1-ounce squares semisweet chocolate. Stir ½ cup egg mixture into chocolate; spread in *baked* 8-inch pastry shell. Cover surface of remaining egg mixture with waxed paper; cool 30 minutes. Drain one 16-ounce can pitted dark sweet cherries; halve cherries and place cut side down on chocolate, reserving 8 halves. Spread cooled mixture over; chill. Whip ½ cup whipping cream; spoon atop pie. Garnish with reserved cherry halves.

Lemon Layer Date Pie

Fancy three-layer pie consists of sweet date bottom, lemon center, and a whipped dessert topping—

>   1 cup snipped pitted dates
>   ¼ cup honey
>   ¼ cup water
>   1 tablespoon lemon juice
>   ⅓ cup chopped walnuts
>   1 baked 9-inch pastry shell
>   • • •
>   1 3¼- or 3⅝-ounce package regular
>   lemon pudding mix
>   ⅓ cup sugar
>   2¼ cups water
>   1 beaten egg
>   • • •
>   1 2-ounce package dessert
>   topping mix

In saucepan combine dates, honey, ¼ cup water, and lemon juice. Bring to boiling. Reduce heat; simmer 10 minutes, stirring often. Add nuts; cool. Turn into pastry shell.

In saucepan combine pudding mix and sugar; stir in 2¼ cups water. Add egg. Cook and stir till thickened and bubbly; cook 2 minutes more. Cover with waxed paper; cool without stirring. Pour over date mixture in shell. Cool. Prepare topping mix following package directions; spread atop. Chill.

Cheese-Topped Pumpkin Pie

Have a pie and cake, too. Pumpkin pie has a dreamy, smooth cheesecake topper—

In large bowl thoroughly combine 1½ cups canned or mashed cooked pumpkin, ¾ cup sugar, 1 teaspoon pumpkin pie spice, ½ teaspoon salt, and ½ teaspoon ground ginger. Blend in 2 slightly beaten eggs, 1¼ cups milk, and 1 teaspoon vanilla. Pour into one unbaked 9-inch pastry shell with edges fluted high.

In mixing bowl combine one 8-ounce package cream cheese, softened; ¼ cup sugar; 1 teaspoon vanilla; and dash salt. Beat in 2 eggs, one at a time. Pour evenly over pumpkin mixture in pastry shell. Bake at 400° till knife inserted just off-center comes out clean, 35 to 40 minutes. Chill. Before serving, garnish top of pie with pecan halves.

Squash Pie

This pie will remind you of pumpkin pie—

In mixing bowl combine 2 cups mashed cooked squash; ½ cup sugar; 1 tablespoon butter or margarine, melted; ½ teaspoon salt; ½ teaspoon ground cinnamon; ¼ teaspoon ground ginger; and ⅛ teaspoon ground nutmeg. Stir in 1¾ cups milk and 2 slightly beaten eggs. Pour mixture into an unbaked 9-inch pastry shell with the edges crimped high. Bake at 400° till knife inserted just off-center comes out clean, about 50 minutes. (Filling may seem soft.) Cool well.

Chocolate Truffle Pie

In saucepan heat 2 cups milk and two 1-ounce squares unsweetened chocolate, broken, over medium-low heat, stirring till blended. In bowl combine 1 cup sugar, ¼ cup cornstarch, and ¼ teaspoon salt. Beat 2 eggs just till blended; add to sugar mixture along with 1½ teaspoons vanilla. Stir to blend. Gradually stir in chocolate mixture. Pour into one unbaked 9-inch pastry shell. Bake at 400° about 35 minutes, covering crust with foil during last 10 to 15 minutes. Cool. (Filling will thicken somewhat on cooling.) Garnish with dollops of whipped cream.

Custard Peach Pie

Sour cream and cream cheese add smoothness—

    1 21-ounce can peach pie filling
    1 8¼-ounce can crushed pineapple,
        drained
    1 baked 9-inch pastry shell
            • • •
    1 cup dairy sour cream
    1 3-ounce package cream cheese,
        softened
    2 slightly beaten eggs
    ⅓ cup sugar

Combine pie filling and pineapple; turn into baked pastry shell. Beat together sour cream and cream cheese; add eggs and sugar, beating till smooth. Pour over peach mixture. Bake at 375° till set, 30 to 35 minutes.

Cherry-Burgundy Pie

Perfect for very special occasions. The cherry filling is sparked with Burgundy—

    1 16-ounce can pitted dark sweet
        cherries
    1 3-ounce package cherry-flavored
        gelatin
    1 pint vanilla ice cream
            • • •
    3 tablespoons red Burgundy
    1 teaspoon lemon juice
    1 baked 8-inch pastry shell

Drain pitted cherries, reserving cherry syrup. Add enough water to syrup to make 1 cup liquid. In saucepan heat liquid to boiling. Dissolve cherry-flavored gelatin in boiling liquid. Spoon vanilla ice cream into gelatin mixture; stir till melted. Blend in wine and lemon juice. Chill till mixture mounds.

Quarter cherries; fold into gelatin mixture. Chill again, if necessary, before piling into baked pastry shell. Chill till firm. Trim with whipped cream, if desired.

Date-Nut-Ice Cream Pie

This festive three-layer pie is perfect for the holidays or served with coffee for bridge club—

    1 quart vanilla ice cream
    1 baked 9-inch pastry shell
    1⅓ cups snipped pitted dates
    ¾ cup water
    1 tablespoon sugar
    1 tablespoon lemon juice
    1 teaspoon vanilla
    ¼ cup chopped walnuts
    2 cups frozen whipped dessert topping,
        thawed

Stir ice cream to soften; spread softened ice cream in bottom of baked pastry shell. Place in freezer. Freeze till firm. Meanwhile, in saucepan combine snipped dates, water, and sugar; cook, covered, till dates are softened, about 5 minutes. Stir in lemon juice and vanilla; cool. Spread *half* of date mixture over ice cream in pastry shell. Fold remaining date mixture and walnuts into whipped topping; spoon over date layer. Freeze till firm.

Serving tiny Lemon-Sour Cream Tarts for dessert ends any meal on a high note. Each person gets his own pie topped with glazed crimson raspberries. Little tart shells are easy to make with piecrust mix.

Tutti-Frutti Parfait Pie

    1 16-ounce can fruit cocktail
      Water
    1 3-ounce package orange-flavored
      gelatin
    1 pint vanilla ice cream
    1 baked 8-inch pastry shell

Drain fruit cocktail, reserving syrup. Add enough water to syrup to make 1¼ cups liquid; heat. Dissolve gelatin in hot liquid. Spoon ice cream into gelatin mixture; stir till melted. Chill mixture till it thickens and mounds when spooned, 40 to 45 minutes. Set aside ½ cup fruit cocktail for garnish. Fold remainder into gelatin-ice cream mixture; turn into pastry shell. Chill till firm. Garnish with reserved fruit cocktail.

Lemon-Sour Cream Tarts

Mix one 18-ounce can lemon pudding and 1 cup dairy sour cream; chill. Drain one 10-ounce package frozen raspberries, thawed, reserving ⅔ cup syrup. Mix 2 tablespoons sugar and 1 tablespoon cornstarch; gradually stir in reserved syrup. Cook and stir till thick and bubbly; chill. Prepare Tart Shells. Fill Tart Shells with lemon mixture; top with a few raspberries. Spoon about 1 tablespoon raspberry glaze over each. Makes 10 tarts.

Tart Shells: Prepare 3 sticks piecrust mix according to package directions. Roll *half* the dough ⅛ inch thick; cut into five 5-inch circles. Repeat with remaining pastry. Fit into tart pans. Trim ½ inch beyond edge; turn under and flute. Prick bottom and sides with fork. Bake at 450° for 10 to 12 minutes; cool.

Plain Pastry

For one single-crust pie or 4 to 6 tart shells —

  1½ cups all-purpose flour
  ½ teaspoon salt
  ½ cup shortening
  4 to 5 tablespoons cold water

For one double-crust or lattice-top pie, two single-crust pies, or 6 to 8 tart shells —

  2 cups all-purpose flour
  1 teaspoon salt
  ⅔ cup shortening
  5 to 7 tablespoons cold water

In mixing bowl stir flour and salt together thoroughly; cut in shortening with pastry blender till pieces are the size of small peas. (For extra-tender pastry, cut in *half* the shortening till like cornmeal. Cut in remaining till like small peas.) Sprinkle 1 tablespoon water over part of mixture. Gently toss with fork; push to side of bowl. Repeat till all is moistened.

Form into a ball. (For double-crust and lattice-top pies, divide dough in half and form into balls.) Flatten on lightly floured surface. Roll from center to edge till ⅛ inch thick.

To bake single-crust pie shells: Fit pastry into 8-, 9-, or 10-inch pie plate; trim ½ to 1 inch beyond edge. Fold under; flute edge by pressing dough with forefinger against wedge made of finger and thumb of other hand. Prick bottom and sides well with fork. (If filling and crust are baked together, *do not prick.*) Bake at 450° till golden, 10 to 12 minutes.

For lattice-top pie: Trim lower crust ½ inch beyond edge of 8-, 9-, or 10-inch pie plate. Roll remaining dough ⅛ inch thick. Cut strips of pastry ½ to ¾ inch wide with pastry wheel or knife. Lay strips on filled pie at 1-inch intervals. Fold back alternate strips to center. Lay one strip crosswise. Return folded strips to original position. Repeat with alternate strips to complete lattice. Trim lattice even with outer rim of pie plate; fold lower crust over strips. Seal; flute edge.

For double-crust pie: Trim lower crust even with rim of 8-, 9-, or 10-inch pie plate. Cut slits in top crust. Lift pastry by rolling it over rolling pin. Then unroll loosely over filled pie. Trim ½ inch beyond edge. Tuck top crust under edge of lower crust. Flute edge.

Yogurt Pastry

Delicate pastry shell contains 662 calories —

  ⅔ cup all-purpose flour
  3 tablespoons shortening
  3 tablespoons plain yogurt

Stir flour and ¼ teaspoon salt together; cut in shortening till pieces are size of small peas. Add yogurt. Gently stir with fork till moistened. Form into a ball. Flatten on lightly floured surface. Roll ⅛ inch thick. Fit pastry into 8-inch pie plate; flute edges. Prick well with fork. Bake at 450° till golden, about 10 minutes.

Electric Mixer Pastry

Measure ¼ cup cold water, ½ cup shortening, 1¼ cups instant-type flour, and ½ teaspoon salt. Mix at low speed of electric mixer till dough begins to form, 15 to 30 seconds. Form into ball. Roll and finish as in Plain Pastry. Makes one 8- or 9-inch single-crust pie.

Oil Pastry

Stir 2 cups all-purpose flour and 1 teaspoon salt together. Pour ½ cup cooking oil and ¼ cup cold milk in measuring cup (do not stir). Add all at once to flour mixture. Stir lightly with fork. Form into 2 balls; flatten slightly.

Between two 12-inch squares waxed paper, roll dough in circle to edge of paper. (First dampen table to prevent slipping.) Peel off top paper and fit dough, paper side up, into pie plate. Remove paper. Finish as in Plain Pastry. Makes one 8- or 9-inch double-crust pie.

Egg Pastry

Stir 4 cups all-purpose flour, 1 tablespoon sugar, and 2 teaspoons salt together thoroughly. Cut in 1½ cups shortening. Combine 1 beaten egg, ½ cup cold water, and 1 tablespoon vinegar; sprinkle over flour mixture, 1 tablespoon at a time. Gently toss with fork; push to side of bowl. Repeat till all is moistened. Store extras in refrigerator in tightly covered container. Makes four 9-inch pastry shells.

Pastry and piecrust pointers

● Measure pastry ingredients accurately. Do not use more or less of an ingredient than is indicated in recipe. Avoid over-mixing the ingredients.
● For perfect pastry circles, press ball of dough with the edge of your hand three times in both directions before rolling. Roll dough to ⅛-inch thickness, rolling from center to edges with light strokes.
● Transfer rolled dough to pie plate by folding in half and placing fold across center of plate, or roll it up on rolling pin and unroll it over the pie plate.
● Ease pastry into pie plate; stretching causes pastry to shrink during baking.
● Shape crumb crusts evenly with an 8-inch pie plate inserted in 9-inch pie plate over crumb mixture; press firmly.
● Bake crumb crusts or chill them thoroughly before adding the filling.

Pecan Pastry

Prepare Plain Pastry (see recipe, page 50) for single-crust pie, *except* add 3 tablespoons finely chopped pecans before adding water. Roll and bake pastry as directed.

Lemon Pastry

Prepare Plain Pastry (see recipe, page 50), *except* add ½ teaspoon grated lemon peel to dry ingredients and substitute 1 tablespoon lemon juice for 1 tablespoon of the cold water. Roll and bake pastry as directed.

Chocolate Wafer Crust

**1½ cups finely crushed chocolate wafers
6 tablespoons butter or margarine, melted**

Combine crushed wafers and melted butter. Press into 9-inch pie plate. Chill till set.

Graham Cracker Crust

**1¼ cups finely crushed graham crackers
6 tablespoons butter, melted
¼ cup sugar**

Combine crushed crackers, melted butter, and sugar. Press into 9-inch pie plate. For unbaked crust, chill 45 minutes. For baked crust, bake at 375° till browned, 6 to 8 minutes; cool.

Vanilla Wafer Crust

**1½ cups finely crushed vanilla wafers
    (36 wafers)
6 tablespoons butter, melted**

Combine crushed wafers and melted butter or margarine. Press into 9-inch pie plate. Chill.

Zwieback Crust

**1 cup crushed zwieback
¼ cup sifted powdered sugar
2 tablespoons butter, melted**

Combine crushed zwieback, powdered sugar, and melted butter or margarine. Press firmly into buttered 8-inch pie plate. Chill.

Coconut Crust

**1 3½-ounce can flaked coconut
    (1⅓ cups)
2 tablespoons butter, melted**

Combine coconut and melted butter. Press firmly into 9-inch pie plate. Bake at 325° till coconut is golden, about 15 minutes.

Gingersnap Crust

**1½ cups finely crushed gingersnaps
¼ cup butter or margarine, softened**

Combine crushed gingersnaps and softened butter. Press firmly into buttered 9-inch pie plate. Bake at 375° about 8 minutes. Cool.

Puddings

Butterscotch Crunch

In saucepan combine ¾ cup packed brown sugar, 2 tablespoons cornstarch, and ¼ teaspoon salt; stir in 2 cups milk. Cook and stir till thickened and bubbly. Cook 2 minutes more; remove from heat. Stir a moderate amount of hot mixture into 2 slightly beaten egg yolks (or 1 well-beaten whole egg); return to hot mixture. Cook and stir till just boiling. Remove from heat; stir in 2 tablespoons butter or margarine and 1 teaspoon vanilla. Cover; cool.

Crush two 1⅛-ounce chocolate-coated English toffee bars; add ¼ cup toasted flaked coconut. In 4 sherbet dishes, alternate pudding and coconut mixture. Makes 4 servings.

Lemon Creme Parfaits

    1 3- or 3¼-ounce package regular
        lemon pudding mix
    ½ cup sugar
    1 cup unsweetened pineapple juice
    2 slightly beaten egg yolks
    1 cup whipping cream
    1 pint fresh or frozen strawberries
    6 ladyfingers, halved lengthwise
        and crosswise

Combine pudding mix and sugar. Gradually blend in juice, yolks, and 1½ cups water. Cook and stir till thick and bubbly. Cool, stirring occasionally. Whip cream to soft peaks; fold into pudding mixture. Chill. Divide *half* pudding mixture among 6 parfait glasses. Reserve 6 berries; spoon remainder into parfaits. Top with remaining pudding. Place ladyfingers around edge. Top with reserved berries. Serves 6.

Creamy candy bar treat

← *Dip your spoon into luscious* Butterscotch Crunch *and enjoy the surprise flavor of chocolate-coated English toffee bars layered with creamy pudding.*

Apricot Macaroon Pudding

Only 147 calories per serving—

    1 cup dried apricots
    2 tablespoons sugar
    1 4-serving envelope low-
        calorie vanilla pudding mix
    1½ cups reconstituted nonfat dry milk
    ⅔ cup coarse dry bread crumbs
    2 tablespoons flaked coconut, toasted

Cook apricots using package directions; stir in sugar. Cool and drain, reserving ½ cup syrup. Dice apricots. Combine pudding mix, milk, and reserved syrup in saucepan; cook and stir till thick and bubbly. Cool slightly. Add crumbs and apricots to pudding mixture; mix well. Spoon into sherbet dishes; sprinkle *each* with 1 teaspoon coconut. Serves 6.

Upside-Down Date Pudding

    1 cup snipped pitted dates
    1 cup boiling water
    ½ cup granulated sugar
    ½ cup packed brown sugar
    1 egg
    2 tablespoons butter, melted
    1½ cups all-purpose flour
    1 teaspoon baking soda
    ½ teaspoon baking powder
    ½ cup chopped walnuts
    1½ cups packed brown sugar
    1½ cups boiling water
    1 tablespoon butter or margarine
        Vanilla ice cream

Combine dates and 1 cup boiling water; cool. Mix next 4 ingredients. Stir together flour, soda, baking powder, and ½ teaspoon salt; add to sugar mixture. Stir in walnuts and date mixture. Pour into 11x7x1½-inch baking pan.

Combine 1½ cups brown sugar, 1½ cups boiling water, and 1 tablespoon butter; pour over date mixture. Bake at 375° for 40 minutes. Serve warm with ice cream. Serves 9 to 12.

Vanilla Pudding

¾ cup granulated sugar
2 tablespoons cornstarch
2 cups milk
2 slightly beaten egg yolks
    or 1 well-beaten egg
2 tablespoons butter or margarine
1 teaspoon vanilla

In saucepan combine sugar, cornstarch, and ¼ teaspoon salt; add milk. Cook and stir over medium heat till thickened and bubbly. Cook and stir 2 minutes more. Remove from heat.

Stir small amount of hot mixture into beaten egg yolks *or* beaten egg. Return to hot mixture; cook and stir 2 minutes more. Remove from heat; add butter and vanilla. Pour into sherbets; chill. Makes 4 or 5 servings.

Chocolate Pudding

Follow directions for Vanilla Pudding, *except* increase sugar to 1 cup and add two 1-ounce squares unsweetened chocolate with milk.

Butterscotch Pudding

Follow directions for Vanilla Pudding, *except* substitute brown sugar for the granulated sugar and increase butter to 3 tablespoons.

Fluffy Tapioca Pudding

4 cups milk
½ cup sugar
¼ cup quick-cooking tapioca
3 slightly beaten egg yolks
1½ teaspoons vanilla
3 stiffly beaten egg whites

Combine milk, sugar, tapioca, and ¼ teaspoon salt; let stand 5 minutes. Add yolks. Bring to boiling, stirring constantly. Remove from heat (mixture will be thin); stir in vanilla. Put *one-third of beaten egg whites* in large bowl; slowly stir in tapioca mixture. Fold in remaining egg whites, leaving little 'pillows' of egg white. Chill. Serves 8 to 10.

Snowy Orange Tapioca

Diet dessert contains 102 calories per serving—

2 egg whites
3 tablespoons sugar
2 tablespoons quick-cooking tapioca
⅛ teaspoon salt
1⅔ cups skim milk
    Few drops vanilla
1 egg white
1 tablespoon sugar
1 medium orange, peeled, chopped,
    and drained

· DIET DESSERT ·
· DIET DESSERT ·

In saucepan combine 2 egg whites, 3 tablespoons sugar, tapioca, and salt; blend in milk. Cook over medium heat, stirring constantly, till mixture comes to full boil, about 10 minutes. Remove from heat; stir in vanilla.

In small mixer bowl beat 1 egg white till foamy. Gradually add 1 tablespoon sugar; continue beating to soft peaks. Gently fold in a few tablespoons of hot tapioca till blended. Gradually fold mixture into remaining tapioca. Cool mixture 15 minutes; fold in chopped orange. Spoon into serving dishes. Chill thoroughly before serving. Serves 5.

Ginger-Mince Pudding

1 package gingerbread mix
¾ cup water
½ cup prepared mincemeat
    Peachy Mince Sauce

Combine gingerbread mix and water; beat with electric mixer for 2 minutes, adding the mincemeat. Turn into greased and lightly floured 9x9x2-inch baking pan. Bake at 350° for 35 to 40 minutes. Serve warm pudding with warm Peachy Mince Sauce. Serves 8.

Peachy Mince Sauce: Drain one 16-ounce can peach slices, reserving syrup. Add enough water to reserved syrup to equal 1 cup liquid. Combine ¼ cup sugar, 1 tablespoon cornstarch, and ¼ teaspoon salt. Stir in reserved peach syrup. Cook, stirring constantly, till thick and bubbly. Add 2 tablespoons butter or margarine, ¼ teaspoon grated lemon peel, and 1 tablespoon lemon juice. Stir in peaches and ½ cup prepared mincemeat. Serve warm.

Pineapple Pudding Cake

>   1 8¾-ounce can crushed pineapple
>   1 package 1-layer-size yellow cake mix
>   • • •
>   1 3-ounce package cream cheese,
>   softened
> 1½ cups milk
>   1 3⅝- or 3¾-ounce package instant
>   vanilla pudding mix
>   1 2-ounce package dessert topping mix

Drain pineapple, reserving syrup. Prepare cake mix according to package directions, *except* substitute reserved pineapple syrup plus enough water to equal liquid called for. Pour into greased and floured 9x9x2-inch baking pan. Bake at 350° for 25 to 30 minutes; cool.

Beat cream cheese with electric mixer till fluffy; gradually beat in milk. Add pudding mix; beat 2 minutes at low speed. Fold in pineapple. Spread atop cake; chill. Prepare topping mix according to package directions. Cut cake in squares; top with topping. Serves 9.

Blueberry Steamed Pudding

Cream 1 cup sugar and ½ cup butter. Mix in 2 eggs and ½ teaspoon vanilla. Stir together 2 cups all-purpose flour, 3 teaspoons baking powder, ½ teaspoon salt, and ½ teaspoon ground cinnamon. Add dry ingredients alternately with ¾ cup milk to butter-egg mixture; mix well. Stir in 2 tablespoons lemon juice.

Carefully fold 1½ cups fresh blueberries into batter. Pour into well-greased and floured 5½-cup mold; cover with foil and tie with string. Place on rack in deep kettle. Add boiling water to depth of 1 inch. Cover; steam 2 hours, adding water if needed. Cool 20 minutes; unmold. Slice, if desired. Serve warm with Blueberry Sauce. Makes 8 servings.

Blueberry Sauce: Combine ½ cup sugar, 1 tablespoon cornstarch, ⅛ teaspoon ground nutmeg, and dash salt. Gradually stir in ½ cup boiling water. Cook, stirring constantly, till thick and bubbly; cook and stir 2 minutes more. Stir in 1 cup fresh blueberries; return to boiling and cook just till berries begin to pop. Remove from heat; stir in 1 tablespoon lemon juice. Makes 1½ cups sauce.

Rice Pudding

This all-time favorite, with or without the raisins, is delicious smothered with cream—

> 2½ cups milk
>   ½ cup long grain rice
>   ⅓ cup sugar
>   ⅓ cup raisins (optional)
>   1 teaspoon vanilla
>   ½ teaspoon salt
>   Light Cream (optional)

In heavy 1½-quart saucepan combine milk, uncooked rice, sugar, raisins (if desired), vanilla, and salt. Bring to boiling. Reduce heat and cook, covered, over very low heat till rice is tender and milk is absorbed, 45 to 50 minutes; stir frequently. Serve with light cream, if desired. Makes 4 servings.

Cottage Pudding

Serve warm for best flavor—

>   ½ cup shortening
>   ¾ cup sugar
>   1 egg
>   ¼ teaspoon lemon extract
> 1¾ cups all-purpose flour
> 2½ teaspoons baking powder
>   ½ teaspoon salt
>   ⅔ cup milk
>   Lemon Sauce

In mixing bowl cream shortening and sugar; add egg and lemon extract. Beat well. Stir together thoroughly flour, baking powder, and salt. Add to creamed mixture alternately with milk, beating after each addition. Spoon into lightly greased and floured 9x9x2-inch baking pan. Bake at 350° till done, 40 to 45 minutes. Serve warm with Lemon Sauce. Serves 9.

Lemon Sauce: In saucepan combine ½ cup sugar, 4 teaspoons cornstarch, dash ground nutmeg, and dash salt. Gradually stir in 1 cup water. Cook, stirring constantly, over low heat till thickened and bubbly. Stir a little hot mixture into 2 beaten egg yolks; return to remaining hot mixture. Cook and stir 1 minute. Remove from heat. Stir in 2 tablespoons butter or margarine, ½ teaspoon grated lemon peel, and 2 tablespoons lemon juice.

Mock Indian Pudding

2 slightly beaten eggs
½ cup light molasses
¼ cup sugar
1 tablespoon butter or margarine, melted
½ teaspoon ground cinnamon
¼ teaspoon salt
¼ teaspoon ground cloves
4 cups cornflakes, coarsely crushed
3 cups milk
1 pint vanilla ice cream

Combine first 7 ingredients; mix well. Stir in cornflake crumbs and milk. Pour into greased 1½-quart casserole. Place in shallow pan on oven rack; pour hot water around casserole in pan to depth of 1 inch. Bake at 350° till knife inserted just off-center comes out clean, about 1 hour. Serve warm with ice cream. Serves 6.

Decked with holly and perfectly traditional for the holidays, the once-a-year dessert treat, American Plum Pudding, *is served with sweet* Foamy Sauce.

Graham Cracker-Prune Pudding

Also good served warm with vanilla ice cream—

Cover 1 cup snipped pitted prunes with boiling water; let stand till cool. Drain. Cream together ⅓ cup sugar, ¼ cup shortening, and 1 teaspoon vanilla; add 1 egg yolk, beating well. Stir in prunes and ¼ cup chopped walnuts.

Mix together 2 cups finely crushed graham crackers, 1 teaspoon baking powder, and ¼ teaspoon salt. Add to creamed mixture alternately with ⅔ cup milk. Fold in 1 stiffly beaten egg white. Fill six 5-ounce greased custard cups. Bake at 350° for 30 minutes. Serve warm with whipped cream. Makes 6 servings.

American Plum Pudding

A traditional Christmas favorite—

2 cups soft bread crumbs
½ cup milk
2 beaten eggs
½ cup packed brown sugar
½ cup chopped suet (3 ounces)
½ cup all-purpose flour
½ teaspoon baking soda
½ teaspoon ground nutmeg
½ teaspoon ground cinnamon
¼ teaspoon salt
1 cup finely chopped, peeled apple
1 cup raisins
¼ cup mixed candied fruits and peels
½ cup finely chopped walnuts
Foamy Sauce

Soak the bread in milk; beat smooth. Stir in eggs, brown sugar, and suet. Stir together flour, soda, spices, and salt. Add fruits and nuts; mix well. Stir in bread mixture. Oil and lightly flour a 1-quart covered mold. Press pudding into mold. Cover with foil; tie with string. Place on rack in deep kettle; add boiling water to depth of 1 inch. Cover and steam till done, about 2 hours, keeping the water boiling. Serve with Foamy Sauce. Serves 6 to 8.

Foamy Sauce: Beat 2 egg whites to stiff peaks; gradually add 1 cup sifted powdered sugar. Beat 2 egg yolks and ¼ teaspoon vanilla till thick; fold into egg whites. In small bowl, whip ½ cup whipping cream to soft peaks; fold into egg mixture.

Pumpkin Rice Pudding

    1 16-ounce can pumpkin
    ¾ cup sugar
    1 teaspoon ground cinnamon
    ½ teaspoon salt
    ½ teaspoon ground ginger
    ¼ teaspoon ground cloves
    2 slightly beaten eggs
    1 14½-ounce can evaporated milk
    ⅔ cup uncooked packaged precooked
        rice
    ½ cup raisins

In mixing bowl combine pumpkin, sugar, ground cinnamon, salt, ground ginger, and ground cloves; stir in eggs. Add evaporated milk, mixing well. Stir in rice and raisins. Pour mixture into a 1½-quart casserole. Place in shallow pan on oven rack; pour hot water around casserole in pan to depth of 1 inch. Bake at 350° for 15 minutes; stir mixture till well combined. Bake till knife inserted just off-center comes out clean, 50 to 60 minutes more. (Or spoon into six to eight 5-ounce custard cups; place in pan. Fill pan with hot water to depth of 1 inch. Bake at 350° till knife inserted just off-center comes out clean, 25 to 30 minutes.) Top with whipped cream or ice cream, if desired. Serves 6 to 8.

Bread Pudding

    2¼ cups milk
    2 slightly beaten eggs
    1 teaspoon vanilla
    ½ teaspoon ground cinnamon
    ¼ teaspoon salt
    2 slices day-old bread, cut in 1 inch
        cubes (2 cups)
    ½ cup packed brown sugar
    ½ cup raisins

Combine milk, eggs, vanilla, cinnamon, and salt; stir in bread cubes. Stir in brown sugar and raisins. Pour mixture into 8x1¾-inch round baking dish. Place dish in larger shallow pan on oven rack; pour hot water into larger pan to depth of 1 inch. Bake at 350° till knife inserted just off-center comes out clean, about 45 minutes. Makes 6 servings.

Orange Creme Brûlee

Drain one 11-ounce can mandarin orange sections. Add 2 tablespoons orange-flavored liqueur; chill. Scald 1⅓ cups light cream. Beat 2 eggs with 3 tablespoons granulated sugar and dash salt till well blended. Gradually stir in hot cream. Place in top of double boiler and cook over *hot, not boiling water*, stirring constantly, till mixture coats a metal spoon in a thick layer, about 15 minutes. (Upper pan should not touch water.) Remove from heat; stir in ¼ cup chopped, toasted almonds, 1 tablespoon orange-flavored liqueur, and ½ teaspoon vanilla. Turn into four 4- or 5-ounce individual soufflé dishes. Chill.

At serving time, sift ⅓ cup packed light brown sugar evenly over pudding by pressing the sugar through sieve. (Brown sugar should make a ¼-inch layer all over pudding. Be sure pudding is completely covered, or it may become watery after broiling.) Set in ovenproof dish of cracked ice and broil 3 to 4 inches from heat just till sugar caramelizes. (This takes only a few seconds.) Top with drained mandarin orange sections. Makes 4 servings.

Apple Bread Pudding

All-time favorite is 128 calories per serving—

    4 slices bread, toasted
    1½ cups reconstituted nonfat dry
        milk
    2 eggs
    ⅓ cup sugar
    ¼ cup raisins
    1 apple, peeled, cored, and diced
    ½ teaspoon ground cinnamon
    ¼ teaspoon salt
    ¼ teaspoon ground nutmeg
    1 tablespoon packed brown sugar

Cut bread into ½-inch cubes. Turn into 9x9x2-inch baking dish. Heat milk; pour over bread and let stand 20 minutes. Beat eggs till light; add sugar, raisins, apple, cinnamon, salt, and nutmeg. Stir into bread mixture. Sprinkle brown sugar over. Place casserole in larger shallow pan on oven rack. Pour hot water around casserole in pan to depth of 1 inch. Bake at 350° for 65 minutes. Serves 8.

Saucy Pomegranate Floating Island

See this pictured on pages 22 and 23. Serve the sauce over ice cream and fruits also—

> 2 egg whites
> ¾ cup sugar
> 3 cups milk
> 3 eggs
> 2 egg yolks
> 1½ teaspoons vanilla
>   Pomegranate Sauce

Beat egg whites with dash salt till soft peaks form. Gradually add ¼ *cup* sugar, beating to stiff peaks. In skillet heat milk to simmering. Drop egg white mixture onto milk in 6 mounds. Cook slowly, uncovered, till set, about 5 minutes. Lift from milk (reserve milk for custard); drain on paper toweling.

In top of double boiler beat eggs and egg yolks slightly; stir in remaining sugar and dash salt. Stir in 3 cups slightly cooled milk (reserved milk plus extra). Place over *hot, not boiling* water. (Upper pan should not touch water.) Cook and stir till mixture coats metal spoon. Remove from heat; cool quickly. Stir in vanilla. Pour custard into serving dish; top with meringues. Pour Pomegranate Sauce over. Makes 6 servings.

Pomegranate Sauce: In saucepan mix 2 cups pomegranate seeds (2 medium pomegranates) and 1 cup water. Cover and simmer 30 minutes; sieve. (Press seeds with hands against sieve to remove all liquid.) Add water to pomegranate juice, if necessary, to equal 1 cup liquid. In saucepan combine 2 tablespoons sugar and 2 teaspoons cornstarch; stir in pomegranate liquid. Cook and stir over medium heat till thickened and bubbly. Cool.

Testing a custard for doneness

Do you know when a baked custard is done? Insert a thin-bladed knife in the custard, just off-center. If the knife comes out clean, the custard is done. Remove pan or custard cups from pan of hot water immediately to stop cooking.

Harvest Pudding with Satin Sauce

> 1 cup packed brown sugar
> ½ cup shortening
> 2 eggs
> 1¾ cups all-purpose flour
> 1 teaspoon baking powder
> 1 teaspoon baking soda
> 1 teaspoon ground cinnamon
> 1 teaspoon ground ginger
> ¼ teaspoon ground cloves
> ½ cup canned pumpkin
> ¼ cup buttermilk
>   Satin Sauce

Cream together brown sugar and shortening. Add eggs; beat till light and fluffy. Stir together dry ingredients and 1 teaspoon salt. Add to creamed mixture alternately with pumpkin and buttermilk, beating well after each addition. Pour into greased 1½-quart mold. Cover with foil; tie with string. Place on rack in deep kettle; add boiling water 1 inch deep. Cover and steam till wooden pick inserted just off-center comes out clean, about 1 hour and 45 minutes (keep the water boiling). Cool; unmold. Spoon Satin Sauce over; sprinkle with toasted almonds, if desired. Serves 8.

Satin Sauce: Beat 1 egg till foamy. Blend in ¾ cup sifted powdered sugar; 3 tablespoons butter or margarine, melted; ½ teaspoon vanilla; and dash ground nutmeg. Whip ½ cup whipping cream; gently fold into egg mixture. Chill. Makes about 1½ cups.

Applesauce Pudding

Spread 8 slices firm-textured white bread with butter or margarine. If desired, remove crusts. Arrange 4 slices bread, buttered side up, in greased 8x8x2-inch baking dish. Mix one 16-ounce can applesauce, ⅓ cup raisins, 2 tablespoons packed brown sugar, and ½ teaspoon ground cinnamon. Spread over bread.

Cut *each* remaining slice bread into 4 triangles; arrange on filling, covering entire surface. Beat together 2½ cups milk, 2 eggs, 6 tablespoons packed brown sugar, ½ teaspoon vanilla, and ¼ teaspoon salt. Pour over bread. Sprinkle with ground cinnamon. Bake at 350° for 50 to 55 minutes. Serves 6 to 8.

Baked Coffee Custard

Coffee lovers will want seconds—

> **2 eggs**
> **⅓ cup sugar**
> **1½ teaspoons instant coffee powder**
> **Dash salt**
> **1½ cups scalded milk**
> • • •
> **Whipped cream**
> **Slivered almonds, toasted**

Beat eggs slightly. Add sugar, coffee powder, and salt; mix well. Gradually stir in milk. Fill four 5-ounce custard cups; set in a shallow pan on oven rack. Pour hot water around cups in pan to depth of 1 inch. Bake custards at 325° till knife inserted just off-center comes out clean, 45 to 50 minutes. Remove custards from pan of hot water; serve warm or chill till serving time. (To unmold chilled custard, first loosen edge; then slip point of knife down side to let air in. Invert.) At serving time, top with dollop of whipped cream and toasted almonds. Makes 4 servings.

Baked Chocolate Custard

Put this velvety custard in the oven to bake while you are eating dinner—

> **2 cups milk**
> **½ cup semisweet chocolate pieces**
> **3 slightly beaten eggs**
> **¼ cup sugar**
> **1 teaspoon vanilla**
> **⅛ teaspoon salt**
> • • •
> **Whipped cream**
> **Slivered almonds, toasted**

In saucepan combine milk and chocolate pieces; stir over low heat till chocolate melts. Cool slightly. In mixing bowl combine eggs, sugar, vanilla, and salt; gradually stir in chocolate mixture. Pour into six 5-ounce custard cups; set in shallow pan on oven rack. Pour hot water around cups in pan to depth of 1 inch. Bake at 325° till knife inserted just off-center comes out clean, 40 to 45 minutes. Invert custards onto serving dishes; garnish with whipped cream and toasted almonds. Serves 6.

Banana Meringue Pudding

In saucepan combine ⅔ cup sugar, ⅓ cup cornstarch, and ½ teaspoon salt; stir in 3 cups milk. Cook over medium heat till thick and bubbly, stirring constantly. Cook and stir 2 minutes more. Add small amount of hot mixture to 3 beaten egg yolks. Return to remaining hot mixture; cook 2 minutes more, stirring constantly. Stir in 3 tablespoons butter or margarine and 1½ teaspoons vanilla; cover surface of pudding with waxed paper. Cool.

Arrange 10 vanilla wafers, 1½ cups sliced banana, and *half* the pudding mixture in 1½-quart casserole. Repeat layering with another 10 vanilla wafers, 1½ cups sliced banana, and remaining pudding, ending with pudding. Beat 3 egg whites to soft peaks; gradually add ⅓ cup sugar, beating to stiff peaks. Spread over pudding, sealing at edges. Bake at 350° for 12 to 15 minutes. Makes 6 servings.

Chocolate Meringue Pudding

Each generous serving is 143 calories—

> **2 cups reconstituted nonfat dry milk**
> **1 1-ounce square unsweetened chocolate**
> **2 beaten egg yolks**
> **¼ cup sugar**
> **1 teaspoon vanilla**
> **Dash salt**
> **2 slices day-old bread cut in 1-inch cubes (2 cups)**
> **Orange Meringue**

Combine milk and chocolate in saucepan. Cook and stir over low heat till chocolate melts. Combine egg yolks, sugar, vanilla, and salt. Blend in chocolate mixture. Add bread cubes; mix lightly to blend. Turn into six 6-ounce custard cups; set in shallow baking pan. Pour hot water around cups in pan to depth of 1 inch. Bake at 350° till knife inserted comes out clean, 30 to 35 minutes. Remove from oven; top each with a dollop of Orange Meringue. Bake till meringue is lightly browned, 8 to 10 minutes. Makes 6 servings.

Orange Meringue: Beat 2 egg whites till soft peaks form. Gradually add 2 tablespoons sugar, beating till stiff peaks form. Fold in ½ teaspoon grated orange peel.

Cookies

Chocolate Crinkle Cookies

    1 cup butter or margarine
    1⅓ cups sifted powdered sugar
    1 teaspoon vanilla
    2 4-ounce bars sweet cooking
        chocolate, grated (2 cups)
    2 cups all-purpose flour
    ½ cup finely chopped walnuts

Cream butter and sugar. Beat in 2 tablespoons water and vanilla. Add chocolate, flour, and dash salt; mix well. Stir in nuts. Shape into 1-inch balls; place on ungreased cookie sheet. Bake at 325° about 25 minutes. Cool. Sprinkle with powdered sugar, if desired. Makes 72.

Peanut Blossoms

    1 cup granulated sugar
    1 cup packed brown sugar
    1 cup butter or margarine
    1 cup creamy peanut butter
    2 eggs
    ¼ cup milk
    2 teaspoons vanilla
    3½ cups all-purpose flour
    2 teaspoons baking soda
    2 6½-ounce packages milk chocolate
        candies

Cream first 4 ingredients. Beat in eggs, milk, and vanilla. Stir together flour, soda, and 1 teaspoon salt; stir into egg mixture. Shape into balls; roll in additional granulated sugar. Place on ungreased cookie sheet; bake at 375° for 10 to 12 minutes. *Immediately* press a chocolate candy into each. Makes 7 dozen.

Cookies, cookies everywhere

← *You can't choose just one; you will have to try all three. The threesome includes* Peanut Blossoms, Orange Drop Cookies, *and* Jam-Filled Cookies.

Orange Drop Cookies

    1½ cups packed brown sugar
    1 cup butter or margarine
    2 eggs
    1 tablespoon grated orange peel
    1 teaspoon vanilla
    3 cups all-purpose flour
    2 teaspoons baking powder
    1 teaspoon baking soda
    ¾ cup buttermilk
    Orange Icing

Cream sugar and butter; beat in next 3 ingredients till fluffy. Stir together dry ingredients and ½ teaspoon salt; beat into sugar mixture alternately with buttermilk. Bake on ungreased cookie sheet at 350° for 10 to 12 minutes. Frost at once with Orange Icing. Makes 72.

  Orange Icing: Mix 1 tablespoon grated orange peel; 3 tablespoons orange juice; 3 tablespoons butter; 3 cups powdered sugar.

Jam-Filled Cookies

    1 cup butter or margarine
    ½ cup granulated sugar
    ½ cup sifted powdered sugar
    1 egg
    1½ teaspoons vanilla
    2¾ cups all-purpose flour
    ½ teaspoon baking soda
    ½ teaspoon cream of tartar
    Jam Filling

Cream butter and sugars. Beat in egg and vanilla. Stir together dry ingredients; beat into egg mixture. Chill. On floured surface, roll dough to ⅛ inch; cut with floured scalloped cookie cutter. Place ½ teaspoon Jam Filling in center of *half* the cookies. Cut out center of remaining cookies; place over filling. Seal. Bake at 350° for 10 to 12 minutes. Makes 30.

  Jam Filling: Add 1 tablespoon water to ½ cup jam (any flavor); stir in 1 tablespoon cornstarch. Cook and stir till thickened. Cool.

Cookie cues

• Flatten molded cookies with bottom of glass dipped in flour or sugar; criss-crossing with fork tines; or pressing center down firmly with thumb.
• Prevent excess spreading of cookies by chilling dough; dropping onto cooled cookie sheet; baking at correct temperature; and mounding dough when dropped.
• Cookies brown evenly on shiny cookie sheets that measure 2 inches shorter and 2 inches narrower than the oven.
• Cool baked cookies on wire racks to prevent sogginess. Bake remaining batches on a cool cookie sheet.
• Store soft cookies in tightly covered container. Add apple wedge if cookies become dry. Keep crisp cookies in jar with a loose-fitting lid to retain freshness.

Chocolate Crunch Cookies

Flavor and crunch are from a candy bar—

    1 cup shortening
    1 cup packed brown sugar
    ½ cup granulated sugar
    2 eggs
    2 tablespoons milk
    1 teaspoon vanilla
    2 cups all-purpose flour
    1 teaspoon baking soda
    1 teaspoon salt
    ½ cup chopped walnuts
    3 1⅝-ounce bars chocolate-coated
        coconut candy bars, chilled and
        coarsely diced (about 1 cup)

Cream together shortening and sugars. Add eggs, milk, and vanilla; beat till fluffy. Stir together flour, baking soda, and salt; blend into creamed mixture. Stir in nuts; gently fold in candy. Drop from tablespoon 2 inches apart on ungreased cookie sheet. Bake at 375° for 10 to 12 minutes. (*Or*, chill dough 30 minutes; roll into 1-inch balls. Place on ungreased cookie sheet; bake 12 to 14 minutes.) Cool on racks. Makes about 4 dozen.

Lemonade Cookies

    1 cup butter or margarine
    1 cup sugar
    2 eggs
    3 cups all-purpose flour
    1 teaspoon baking soda
    1 6-ounce can frozen lemonade
        concentrate, thawed (⅔ cup)

In large mixer bowl cream butter and sugar. Add eggs, beating till light and fluffy. Stir together flour and soda; add to creamed mixture alternately with ½ *cup* of the lemonade concentrate. Drop from teaspoon onto greased cookie sheet. Bake at 400° for 8 to 10 minutes. Brush hot cookies lightly with remaining lemonade concentrate; sprinkle with a little granulated sugar, if desired. Remove to rack; cool. Makes about 4 dozen cookies.

Cereal Cookies

    1 cup granulated sugar
    1 cup packed brown sugar
    1 cup shortening
    2 eggs
    1 teaspoon vanilla
    2½ cups all-purpose flour
    1 teaspoon cream of tartar
    1 teaspoon baking soda
    ¼ teaspoon salt
    2 cups high-protein rice cereal
        flakes

In bowl cream sugars and shortening. Add eggs and vanilla; beat well. Stir together dry ingredients. Add to creamed mixture and mix well. Stir in cereal. Form into 1-inch balls. Place on ungreased cookie sheet; bake at 375° for 10 minutes. Makes 6 dozen cookies.

Applesauce Cookies

Combine 1 package 2-layer-size spice cake mix, 1 cup raisins, ½ cup cooking oil, ½ cup applesauce, and 1 egg; beat at medium speed of electric mixer for 1 minute. Drop from teaspoon onto ungreased cookie sheet. Bake at 350° for 12 to 15 minutes. Makes 6 dozen.

Butterscotch Cookies

1½ cups packed brown sugar
¾ cup butter or margarine
2 eggs
1 tablespoon vinegar
1 teaspoon vanilla
1 cup evaporated milk
2½ cups all-purpose flour
1 teaspoon baking soda
½ teaspoon baking powder
½ teaspoon salt
1 cup chopped walnuts
Golden Glow Frosting

Cream sugar and butter till light. Add eggs; beat well. Add vinegar and vanilla to evaporated milk. Stir together dry ingredients; stir into creamed mixture alternately with milk. Stir in chopped nuts. Drop by rounded tablespoons 2 inches apart on greased cookie sheet. Bake at 350° till golden brown, 10 to 12 minutes. Cool. Frost with Golden Glow Frosting. Top with walnut half, if desired. Makes 78.

Golden Glow Frosting: In saucepan cook ½ cup butter over medium heat till bubbly and golden. Add 3 cups sifted powdered sugar; stir in enough boiling water to make spreadable (about ¼ cup). Beat till smooth.

Toffee Drop Cookies

1½ cups packed brown sugar
1 cup butter or margarine
2 eggs
¼ cup milk
2 teaspoons vanilla
3½ cups all-purpose flour
1 teaspoon baking powder
1 teaspoon salt
1 teaspoon baking soda
6 1⅛-ounce chocolate-coated
    English toffee bars, chopped

Cream first 5 ingredients till fluffy. Stir together dry ingredients; add to creamed mixture in bowl. Blend well. Stir in *1 cup* chopped candy. Drop dough from teaspoon 2 inches apart on ungreased cookie sheet. Sprinkle with remaining candy. Bake at 375° for 10 to 12 minutes. Makes about 5 dozen cookies.

Macaroons

1 8-ounce can almond paste
1 cup granulated sugar
3 egg whites
⅓ cup sifted powdered sugar
2 tablespoons all-purpose flour

In mixer bowl crumble almond paste; gradually beat in next 2 ingredients. Mix powdered sugar, flour, and ⅛ teaspoon salt; blend into almond-sugar mixture. Drop by teaspoon onto greased cookie sheet, or press through pastry bag, using large rose point. Bake at 300° till light brown, about 25 minutes. Let stand 1 to 2 minutes; cool on rack. Makes 32.

Vanilla Crisps

Each delicate cookie contains 48 calories—

⅔ cup sugar
½ cup butter or margarine
½ cup shortening
2 teaspoons vanilla
2 eggs
2½ cups all-purpose flour

Cream first 3 ingredients. Add vanilla and 1 teaspoon salt. Add eggs, one at a time, beating well after each. Stir in flour; mix well. Drop from teaspoon onto greased cookie sheet. Flatten with floured glass. Bake at 375° till edges are delicately browned, 8 to 10 minutes. Remove immediately from cookie sheet to rack. Makes 6 dozen.

Carmelitas

In top of double boiler over *hot, not boiling* water melt 32 caramels in ¼ cup light cream *or* evaporated milk, stirring till smooth. Slice 1 roll refrigerated chocolate chip cookie dough ¼ inch thick and place on bottom of 9x9x2-inch baking pan, patting to make even crust. Bake at 375° for 25 minutes. Cool slightly. Sprinkle one 6-ounce package semisweet chocolate pieces over warm cookie base; carefully spread caramel mixture atop. Refrigerate 1 to 2 hours; cut into squares. Top with pecan halves. Makes 36 pieces.

Butterscotch Bars

½ cup butter or margarine
2 cups packed brown sugar
2 eggs
1 teaspoon vanilla
2 cups all-purpose flour
2 teaspoons baking powder
1 cup flaked coconut
1 cup chopped peanuts

In saucepan melt butter. Remove from heat; stir in brown sugar. Add eggs, one at a time; beat after each. Add vanilla. Stir together dry ingredients and ¼ teaspoon salt. Stir flour mixture, coconut, and nuts into egg mixture. Spread in greased 15½x10½x1-inch baking pan. Bake at 350° for 25 minutes. Cut bars while warm. Dust with powdered sugar, if desired. Remove when almost cool. Makes 36.

Chocolate-Cream Cheese Brownies

1 4-ounce package German
    sweet chocolate
2 tablespoons butter or margarine
2 eggs
1 teaspoon vanilla
1 cup sugar
½ cup all-purpose flour
½ teaspoon baking powder
½ cup chopped walnuts
1 3-ounce package cream cheese,
    softened
1 egg
½ teaspoon vanilla

Combine chocolate and butter; melt and cool. Beat 2 eggs and 1 teaspoon vanilla; gradually add ¾ *cup* sugar. Beat till thick and lemon-colored. Stir together dry ingredients and ¼ teaspoon salt; add to egg mixture, beating well. Blend in chocolate mixture and nuts.

Cream cheese and remaining sugar till fluffy. Blend in 1 egg and ½ teaspoon vanilla. Spread *half* the chocolate mixture in greased and lightly floured 8x8x2-inch baking pan. Pour cheese mixture over; top with spoonfuls of remaining chocolate mixture. Swirl through layers to marble. Bake at 350° for 40 to 45 minutes. Cut in squares when cool. Makes 16.

Cherry Pineapple Bars

2 cups all-purpose flour
1 cup packed brown sugar
½ teaspoon salt
1 cup butter or margarine
½ cup granulated sugar
2 tablespoons cornstarch
1 8¾-ounce can crushed pineapple
2 beaten egg yolks
1 cup maraschino cherries, chopped

Combine flour, brown sugar, and salt; cut in butter till crumbly. Set aside 1 cup crumb mixture; press remaining mixture on bottom of 13x9x2-inch baking pan. Bake at 350° for 15 minutes. Cool slightly while preparing topping.

In saucepan combine granulated sugar and cornstarch. Stir in undrained pineapple and egg yolks. Cook and stir over medium heat till mixture thickens and bubbles. Remove from heat; stir in cherries. Spread evenly over baked layer. Sprinkle on reserved crumb mixture. Bake at 350° for 30 minutes more. Cool before cutting into bars. Makes 2½ dozen.

Cheesecake Diamonds

Cream cheese gives special smoothness—

5 tablespoons butter or margarine
⅓ cup packed brown sugar
1 cup all-purpose flour
¼ cup chopped walnuts
½ cup granulated sugar
1 8-ounce package cream cheese,
    softened
1 egg
2 tablespoons milk
1 tablespoon lemon juice
½ teaspoon vanilla

Cream butter and brown sugar; add flour and nuts and mix well. Set aside one cup mixture for topping. Press remainder in bottom of 8x8x2-inch baking pan. Bake at 350° for 12 to 15 minutes. Blend granulated sugar and cream cheese till smooth. Add egg, milk, lemon juice, and vanilla. Beat well. Spread over bottom baked crust; sprinkle with the reserved topping. Return to oven; bake 25 minutes more. Cool, then chill. Cut in diamonds. Makes 16.

Tri-Level Brownies

- ½ cup all-purpose flour
- ¼ teaspoon baking soda
- ¼ teaspoon salt
- 1 cup quick-cooking rolled oats
- ½ cup packed brown sugar
- 6 tablespoons butter or margarine, melted
- ¾ cup granulated sugar
- ¼ cup butter or margarine, melted
- 1 1-ounce square unsweetened chocolate, melted and cooled
- 1 egg
- ⅔ cup all-purpose flour
- ¼ teaspoon baking powder
- ¼ teaspoon salt
- ¼ cup milk
- ½ teaspoon vanilla
- ½ cup chopped walnuts
  Perfect Fudge Frosting

Stir together first 3 ingredients; mix with rolled oats and brown sugar. Stir in 6 tablespoons butter. Pat mixture in 11x7x1½-inch baking pan. Bake at 350° for 10 minutes.

Combine granulated sugar, ¼ cup melted butter or margarine, and chocolate; add egg. Beat well. Stir together ⅔ cup flour, baking powder, and ¼ teaspoon salt; add to chocolate mixture alternately with milk and vanilla. Fold in chopped walnuts. Spread batter over baked layer. Return to oven and bake at 350° for 25 minutes more. Spread baked brownies with Perfect Fudge Frosting. Cut in bars. Top with walnut halves, if desired. Makes 16.

Perfect Fudge Frosting: Place one 1-ounce square unsweetened chocolate and 2 tablespoons butter or margarine in small saucepan. Stir over low heat till chocolate melts. Remove from heat and add 1½ cups sifted powdered sugar and 1 teaspoon vanilla. Blend in enough hot water (about 2 tablespoons) to make almost pourable consistency.

Triple brownie special

Treat your morning coffee friends to a platter of Tri-Level Brownies. The kids will also love them after school served with a frosty glass of milk.

Fruit Desserts

Rumtopf

Peel, section, and cut up 3 medium oranges over bowl to catch juice. In crock combine chopped oranges; 3 medium pears, cored and diced; and 1 cup maraschino cherries. Stir in 1 cup sugar; pour in juice from sectioned oranges and 1 cup rum. Cover. Refrigerate for 2 weeks. Serve as compote or over ice cream or cake. (To keep Rumtopf going: For every cup of fruit removed, add 1 cup of fruit, ⅓ cup sugar, and ⅓ cup rum. Keep refrigerated.)

Fruited Gelatin Parfaits

    1 3-ounce package lemon-flavored
        gelatin
    ¼ teaspoon salt
    1 cup boiling water
    ¾ cup cold water
    1 10-ounce package frozen mixed
        fruit
        • • •
    ½ cup lemon yogurt
    2 teaspoons sugar

Dissolve gelatin and salt in boiling water; add cold water. Set aside ½ cup mixture. Add frozen fruit to remaining gelatin mixture, stirring carefully to separate fruit. Chill till *partially* set, 10 to 15 minutes; spoon into 6 parfait glasses. Chill till *nearly* set.

Meanwhile, chill the reserved ½ cup gelatin till *partially* set. Beat with rotary or electric beater till light and fluffy, 1 to 2 minutes. Stir together lemon yogurt and sugar; fold into whipped gelatin. Spoon mixture atop gelatin in parfait glasses. Chill till set. Makes 6 servings.

Seasonal dessert topper

← As various fruits come in season, feature them in Rumtopf. *Get the versatile compote and dessert topper started with fruit chunks, rum, and sugar.*

Berry Parfaits

Layered parfait has 68 calories per serving —

    1 tablespoon sugar
    1 teaspoon grated orange peel
    ½ teaspoon grated lemon peel
    ⅛ teaspoon ground cinnamon
    1 cup plain yogurt
    1½ cups strawberries, sliced
    1½ cups blueberries

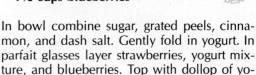

In bowl combine sugar, grated peels, cinnamon, and dash salt. Gently fold in yogurt. In parfait glasses layer strawberries, yogurt mixture, and blueberries. Top with dollop of yogurt mixture and a strawberry slice. Serves 6.

Peach Melba

In saucepan combine 1 cup sugar and 2 cups water. Bring to boiling; reduce heat and simmer, stirring constantly, till sugar is dissolved. Peel and halve 3 peaches; add *half* to sugar mixture. Cover and simmer till tender, about 5 minutes. Remove from syrup. Repeat with remaining peaches. Cool and chill. Top with vanilla ice cream and Raspberry Sauce. Serves 6.

Raspberry Sauce: Thaw and crush one 10-ounce package frozen raspberries. Combine with 1 tablespoon cornstarch. Add ½ cup currant jelly. Cook and stir till bubbly; cook 1 minute more. Strain; cool. Makes 1¼ cups.

Strawberries Continental

    3 pints strawberries
    ⅔ cup orange juice
    ⅔ cup tawny port
    ⅓ cup sugar
    ½ cup whipping cream
    1 tablespoon powdered sugar

Wash and hull berries. Combine with next 3 ingredients. Chill 2 to 3 hours. Whip cream; fold in sugar. Serve atop berries. Serves 8.

Fruit Compote Supreme

    1 16-ounce can peach slices
    1 cup dried apricots
    ½ cup packed brown sugar
    1 teaspoon grated orange peel
    ⅓ cup orange juice
    ½ teaspoon grated lemon peel
    2 tablespoons lemon juice
    1 16-ounce can pitted dark sweet
        cherries, drained

Combine all ingredients except cherries in 10x6x2-inch baking dish. Cover; bake at 350° for 45 minutes. Add cherries; bake, covered, 15 minutes more. Makes 6 to 8 servings.

Creamy Fruit Cup

Each creamy-sauced serving has 121 calories—

    2 egg yolks
    2 tablespoons sugar
    1 teaspoon lemon juice
    ½ teaspoon vanilla
    2 3-ounce packages Neufchâtel
        cheese, softened
    3 tablespoons skim milk
    2 medium bananas
    3 medium peaches
        Ground cinnamon

Beat first 4 ingredients till thick and lemon-colored. Beat in cheese till fluffy. Beat in milk. Chill well. Slice fruits; top with cheese mixture. Sprinkle with cinnamon. Serves 6.

Retain fresh fruit color

Some fresh fruits, such as apples, avocados, nectarines, bananas, peaches, and pears, will darken when cut and exposed to air. To retain a fresh, bright fruit color, dip the cut fruit in orange, lemon, lime, or pineapple juice mixed with water. A special ascorbic acid color keeper also is available and easy to use following label directions.

Cheddar-Topped Poached Apples

Hot cheesy apples pictured on pages 22 and 23—

    ⅓ cup sugar
    ⅓ cup light molasses
    2 tablespoons lemon juice
    ¼ teaspoon ground cinnamon
    ¼ teaspoon ground nutmeg
        Dash ground cloves
        Dash ground ginger
    6 large baking apples, peeled and
        cored
        Cheddar Whip

In medium skillet combine sugar, molasses, juice, spices, and 1 cup water; bring to boil. Reduce heat; add apples. Cover and simmer 10 to 15 minutes, spooning syrup over apples often. Turn apples over and simmer, uncovered, till tender, 5 to 10 minutes. Fill apple centers with Cheddar Whip. Serves 6.

Cheddar Whip: In small mixer bowl combine one 3-ounce package cream cheese, softened; ½ cup shredded natural Cheddar cheese (2 ounces); and 2 tablespoons milk. Beat till smooth.

Mincemeat-Filled Apples

Core 8 large baking apples; peel strip from top of each. Place in 11x7½x1½-inch baking pan; fill centers with 1 cup prepared brandied mincemeat. Pour 1 cup water into dish around apples. Bake, uncovered, at 350° for 50 to 60 minutes. Stir 2 tablespoons brandy into 1 cup frozen whipped dessert topping, thawed; spoon atop warm apples. Serves 8.

Fruited Baked Apples

*Each fruit-filled apple
serving is 134 calories—*

Core 6 small baking apples, enlarging opening slightly to allow for filling. Combine 1 medium banana, chopped; ½ cup cranberries, chopped; ¼ cup honey; and ½ teaspoon ground cinnamon. Fill centers of apples. Place in 12x7½x2-inch baking dish. Pour ½ cup water around apples in dish. Bake at 350° till tender, 50 to 60 minutes. Makes 6 servings.

Bananas aux Fruits

Combine 1 slightly beaten egg and 1 tablespoon lemon juice. Peel 6 firm medium bananas and coat with egg mixture; place on greased baking sheet. Break 9 soft macaroon cookies into coarse crumbs; stir in 2 tablespoons all-purpose flour; pile on bananas. Bake at 375° for 8 to 10 minutes. Combine ¼ cup apricot preserves, 2 tablespoons melted butter, and 2 teaspoons lemon juice; spoon over bananas. Bake till hot, 3 to 5 minutes more. Serve with hot Cherry Sauce. Serves 6.

Cherry Sauce: Drain one 8¾-ounce can pitted dark sweet cherries, reserving syrup. Halve cherries. Add enough port wine to syrup to make ¾ cup. In saucepan combine 2 tablespoons sugar, 1 tablespoon cornstarch, and dash salt. Stir in reserved syrup mixture. Cook, stirring constantly, till mixture thickens and bubbles; add cherries and heat just to boiling.

Cranberry-Pear Compote

Ruby dessert has 88 calories per serving. Good with dessert topping, but remember to add on calories—

- **2 16-ounce cans low-calorie pear halves**
- **1 cup low-calorie jellied cranberry sauce**
- **2 tablespoons sugar**
- **¼ teaspoon ground cinnamon**
- **¼ teaspoon ground ginger**
- **2 medium oranges, peeled, sliced, and halved**

Drain and quarter pears, reserving ¼ cup syrup. Combine cranberry sauce, reserved pear syrup, sugar, cinnamon, and ginger; bring mixture to boiling. Place pear quarters and orange slices in 1½-quart casserole. Pour cranberry mixture over fruit. Cover and bake at 350° for 35 to 40 minutes. Serve warm. Serves 6.

Fancy Bananas aux Fruits *would be a perfect ending to your next dinner party. The golden, baked bananas are crowned with a macaroon and apricot preserve topper and served with a ruby wine-sparked cherry sauce.*

A surprise sherried maraschino cherry filling waits inside each succulent, meringue-topped baked pear. Spoon chocolate sauce over Meringue Pears with Chocolate *right at the table for anxious dessert lovers.*

Peaches in Spiced Wine

Spicy wine-sauced peaches are a delicious treat to anyone at only 62 calories per serving—

   ¼ **cup dry sauterne**
   2 **tablespoons sugar**
   1 **tablespoon lemon juice**
      ● ● ●
     Dash ground cinnamon
     Dash ground cloves
   3 **medium peaches, peeled and sliced**
      (2 cups)

In small saucepan heat together sauterne, sugar, and lemon juice. Cook and stir till sugar dissolves (do not boil). Stir in ground cinnamon and ground cloves. Pour hot wine mixture over sliced peaches in deep bowl. Chill mixture thoroughly. Makes 4 servings.

Meringue Pears with Chocolate

Peel 6 pears; core and trim bottoms. Combine ½ cup water, ¼ cup sugar, ¼ cup apricot jam, 2 tablespoons dry sherry, and 2 teaspoons lemon juice; cook and stir till sugar dissolves. Add pears; cover and simmer till tender, stirring occasionally, about 20 minutes.

Meanwhile, soak 2 tablespoons chopped maraschino cherries in 1 tablespoon dry sherry. Remove pears to shallow baking dish, reserving ½ cup cooking liquid. Fill pear centers with cherries. Beat 1 egg white till soft peaks form; gradually add 3 tablespoons sugar, beating to stiff peaks. Swirl meringue atop each pear. Bake at 350° till browned, about 12 minutes. Add one 1-ounce square semisweet chocolate to reserved liquid; heat and stir till melted. Spoon over pears. Makes 6 servings.

Strawberry Meringue Cake

Party-perfect dessert pictured on page 4—

    1 package 2-layer-size yellow cake mix
    1 teaspoon grated orange peel
    1 cup orange juice
    ⅓ cup water
    4 egg yolks
    4 egg whites
    ¼ teaspoon cream of tartar
    1 cup sugar
    1 quart fresh strawberries
    2 cups whipping cream
    ¼ cup sugar

Combine cake mix, peel, juice, water, and yolks; beat 4 minutes on medium speed of electric mixer. Pour into 2 greased and waxed paper-lined 9x1½-inch round baking pans.

Beat egg whites with cream of tartar to soft peaks; gradually add the 1 cup sugar, beating to stiff peaks. Gently spread meringue evenly over batter. Bake at 350° for 35 to 40 minutes; cool completely. With flexible spatulas, carefully remove layers from pans, keeping meringue side up. Set aside a few berries for garnish; slice remainder. Whip cream with ¼ cup sugar. Spread *two-thirds* of the whipped cream over meringue on bottom cake layer. Arrange sliced berries on whipped cream. Add top layer, meringue side up. Garnish with remaining whipped cream and whole berries.

Pineapple Cake

Broil pineapple topper just before serving—

    1 package 1-layer-size yellow cake mix
         • • •
    1 8¾-ounce can crushed pineapple,
         well drained
    ½ cup flaked coconut
    ⅓ cup packed brown sugar
    3 tablespoons butter or margarine,
         melted

Prepare cake mix according to package directions. Pour into greased and floured 8x8x2-inch baking pan. Bake at 350° for 30 to 35 minutes. Combine remaining ingredients; spread atop cake. Broil 4 to 5 inches from heat till golden, 5 to 7 minutes. Serve warm.

Rhubarb Kuchen à la Mode

    1 cup all-purpose flour
    1 tablespoon sugar
    1½ teaspoons baking powder
    2 tablespoons butter or margarine
    1 egg
    2 tablespoons milk
    1 3-ounce package strawberry-
         flavored gelatin
    ⅓ cup sugar
    3 tablespoons all-purpose flour
    1½ pounds rhubarb, sliced (5 cups)
    ⅔ cup sugar
    ⅓ cup all-purpose flour
    3 tablespoons butter or margarine
         Vanilla ice cream

Stir together first 3 ingredients and ⅛ teaspoon salt. Cut in 2 tablespoons butter till it resembles coarse crumbs. Beat egg with milk; add to flour mixture. Stir till dry ingredients are moistened. Pat evenly on bottom and 1 inch up sides of 9x9x2-inch baking pan.

Combine gelatin, ⅓ cup sugar, and 3 tablespoons flour. Add to rhubarb and mix well; turn into crust-lined pan. Combine ⅔ cup sugar and ⅓ cup flour; cut in the 3 tablespoons butter till crumbly. Sprinkle evenly over rhubarb filling. Bake at 375° till rhubarb is tender and topping is lightly browned, about 45 minutes. Cool completely. Cut into squares; top with ice cream. Makes 8 servings.

Apricot Angel Dessert

In saucepan combine ¾ cup sugar and 1 envelope unflavored gelatin; stir in 2½ cups apricot nectar. Cook and stir till boiling. Stir a moderate amount into 2 slightly beaten eggs; return all to saucepan. Cook and stir till slightly thickened. Chill till partially set.

Slice 9 apricot halves from one drained 17-ounce can apricot halves; set aside. Chop remaining apricots. Whip 1 cup whipping cream; fold into gelatin mixture with chopped apricots. Fold into 9 cups angel cake cubes. Turn mixture into 13x9x2-inch baking pan. Chill several hours or overnight. Cut into squares. Garnish with reserved apricot slices and maraschino cherries. Makes 12 servings.

Low-Calorie Strawberry Tarts

Meringue cup with creamy filling and fruit topping is 132 calories a serving—

    1 4-serving envelope low-calorie vanilla pudding mix
    2 cups reconstituted nonfat dry milk
    ½ teaspoon imitation strawberry extract
    ¼ teaspoon red food coloring
    1 envelope from a 2½-ounce package low-calorie dessert topping mix
    8 Petal Meringue Shells
    1 cup sliced strawberries
    ¾ cup quartered seedless green grapes
    8 meringue stars

Prepare pudding, using the 2 cups reconstituted milk, according to package directions. Stir in extract and food coloring. Cover surface with waxed paper; cool to room temperature. Prepare dessert topping mix according to package directions; fold into pudding. Chill. At serving time, spoon pudding mixture into Petal Meringue Shells. Top with strawberry slices, grapes, and meringue stars. Serves 8.

Petal Meringue Shells: In small mixer bowl beat 2 egg whites, ½ teaspoon vanilla, ¼ teaspoon cream of tartar, and dash salt to soft peaks. Gradually add ½ cup sugar, beating till very stiff peaks form. Place *about ¼ cup* meringue in each of 8 well-greased 3½x1-inch tart pans; with small spatula spread evenly on bottom and sides of pans, bringing meringue to peaks around top edges. Force remaining meringue through pastry tube onto brown-paper-lined baking sheet to make 8 stars. Bake stars at 275° for 30 minutes; bake shells at 275° for 40 to 45 minutes. Remove from oven. Cool; remove meringue shells from pans.

Fruit Toss

Each refreshing fresh fruit serving is only 65 calories—

Mix ½ cup plain yogurt, 1 tablespoon sugar, and ½ teaspoon vanilla. Mix in 2 cups chopped apple; 1 fresh orange, peeled, sectioned, and diced; 1 banana, sliced; and 1½ cups strawberries, halved. Chill. Serves 8.

Strawberry Dumplings

    ⅓ cup sugar
    ⅔ cup water
    ½ teaspoon vanilla
    • • •
    1 cup all-purpose flour
    2 tablespoons sugar
   1½ teaspoons baking powder
    ½ teaspoon salt
    ¼ cup butter or margarine
    ½ cup milk
    1 pint strawberries, hulled
    1 tablespoon sugar

In saucepan combine ⅓ cup sugar and water. Bring mixture to boiling; reduce heat and simmer, uncovered, 5 minutes. Stir in vanilla. Stir together flour, 2 tablespoons sugar, baking powder, and salt. Cut in butter till mixture is crumbly. Add milk and stir just till well combined. Place berries in 1½-quart casserole; pour *hot* sugar mixture over. Immediately drop dumpling dough in 8 to 10 spoonfuls over berries. Sprinkle dumplings with remaining sugar. Bake at 450° till done, 25 to 30 minutes. Serve warm. Makes 4 or 5 servings.

Fresh Rhubarb Betty

    2 oranges
  1¾ cups sugar
    1 tablespoon all-purpose flour
    ¼ teaspoon salt
    5 cups rhubarb, cut in ½-inch pieces (about 1½ pounds)
    4 cups soft bread cubes (5 slices)
    ½ cup butter or margarine, melted
    ½ cup flaked coconut

Grate 1 teaspoon orange peel. Peel, section, and dice oranges; set aside. In mixing bowl combine sugar, flour, salt, and ½ *teaspoon* orange peel. Stir in rhubarb and orange. Add *2 cups* bread cubes and ¼ *cup* melted butter; mix lightly. Turn into 8x8x2-inch baking dish. Combine the remaining bread cubes, melted butter, remaining orange peel, and coconut. Sprinkle over rhubarb mixture. Bake at 375° till golden and rhubarb is tender, 35 to 40 minutes. Serve warm. Serves 6 to 8.

Peaches and Cream Crisp

> 1 29-ounce can peach slices, drained
> ¾ cup quick-cooking rolled oats
> ½ cup packed brown sugar
> ½ cup all-purpose flour
> 6 tablespoons butter or margarine
>   Vanilla ice cream

Arrange drained peach slices in an 8x1½-inch round baking dish. In mixing bowl mix rolled oats, brown sugar, flour, and butter or margarine till crumbly. Sprinkle over peach slices. Bake at 350° for 30 minutes. Serve warm with vanilla ice cream. Makes 6 servings.

Quick Pear Torte

> ¾ cup sugar
> ¼ cup butter or margarine
> 3 eggs
> 1 teaspoon vanilla
> 1 stick piecrust mix, finely crumbled
> 1 cup snipped dried pears
> ½ cup snipped pitted dates
> ½ cup chopped walnuts
>   Vanilla ice cream (optional)

In small mixer bowl cream sugar and butter or margarine. Beat in eggs and vanilla till blended; stir in crumbled piecrust mix. Add snipped dried pears, dates, and walnuts. Turn mixture into greased 8x8x2-inch baking dish. Bake at 325° till done, 40 to 45 minutes. Cut warm dessert in squares to serve; top with vanilla ice cream, if desired. Makes 8 servings.

Brandied Kumquats

This ice cream topper is pictured on page 22—

> 4 cups fresh kumquats
> 1½ cups sugar
> ½ cup brandy

Quarter the kumquats, removing seeds if desired. In medium saucepan combine kumquats and sugar; bring to boiling. Reduce heat; cover and simmer till kumquats are tender, 20 to 25 minutes. Cool slightly; stir in brandy. Cover and store in refrigerator. Makes about 3 cups.

Fresh Tangerine Sherbet

Refreshing ice treat pictured on page 23—

> 3½ cups milk
> 1½ cups sugar
> 1 teaspoon grated tangerine peel
> 1½ cups fresh tangerine juice (5
>   to 6 tangerines)
> 2 tablespoons lemon juice
>   Orange food coloring

In mixing bowl combine all ingredients, stirring till sugar dissolves. Pour into refrigerator tray; freeze till nearly firm. Break into chunks; turn into chilled mixer bowl. Using electric mixer, beat till fluffy with chilled beaters. Turn into 6-cup chilled mold. Freeze firm. Let stand at room temperature 10 to 15 minutes before serving. Serves 8 to 10.

Strawberry Ice

Chilly strawberry dessert is 65 calories a serving—

> 2 10-ounce packages frozen sliced
>   strawberries, thawed (2 cups)
> 1 3-ounce package strawberry-
>   flavored gelatin
> 1 cup boiling water
> 1 tablespoon lemon juice

Purée strawberries in blender. Set aside. Dissolve gelatin in boiling water; stir in lemon juice and 1 cup cold water. Stir in strawberries. Freeze in two 4-cup refrigerator trays. Break into chunks; in chilled bowl beat *half* the mixture with an electric mixer till light and fluffy. Return to tray; repeat with remaining mixture. Freeze firm. Makes 14 servings.

Peach Sundae

*Only 68 calories for each
refreshing serving—*

Peel, pit, and slice 5 peaches. Purée ¾ cup of the peach slices; stir in 2 tablespoons sugar. Spoon remaining peach slices into individual sherbet dishes. Stir ½ cup lemon sherbet to soften; fold in ½ cup plain yogurt and puréed peaches. Drizzle about 3 tablespoons topping over each serving. Makes 8 servings.

Desserts Made Easy

Not enough time to prepare everything? Relax. This section offers an assortment of shortcut and make-ahead specialties. Whip up Peach-Caramel Cobbler for unexpected guests while the coffee perks. Choco-Mo Ice Cream, Fruitcake Soufflés, and Peppermint Ice Cream Roll are excellent make-ahead desserts. (See index for page numbers.)

Shortcut Desserts

Cocoa-Mocha Parfaits

1 4-ounce package chocolate soft-
   style whipped dessert mix
2 tablespoons coffee-flavored liqueur
1 tablespoon crème de cacao
⅓ cup crushed chocolate wafers

Prepare dessert mix according to package directions; fold in liqueurs. Chill mixture till it
mounds. Layer in 4 parfait glasses with chocolate crumbs. Chill till firm. Top with additional
chocolate wafer crumbs and a maraschino
cherry, if desired. Serves 4.

Speedy Strawberry Parfaits

Cream cheese and yogurt enhance strawberry—

1 3-ounce package cream cheese,
   softened
1 cup plain yogurt
¼ cup sugar
1 21-ounce can strawberry pie filling
2 tablespoons chopped almonds, toasted

In small mixer bowl beat together cream
cheese, yogurt, and sugar till smooth. Spoon
alternate layers of yogurt mixture and pie filling into 6 parfait glasses. Top with almonds.
Serve with ladyfingers, if desired. Serves 6.

Cherry Crunch Parfaits

A unique, anytime dessert treat—

Cut ¼ cup butter or margarine into one 1-layer-
size yellow cake mix till mixture resembles
coarse crumbs. Stir in ¼ cup chopped walnuts
and 1 tablespoon water. Press into 9x9x2-inch
baking pan. Bake at 350° till golden, 15 to 20
minutes. Cool till comfortable to handle; crumble. Blend together two 20-ounce cans cherry
pie filling and 2 tablespoons lemon juice.
Layer the crunch mixture and the cherry pie
filling into 8 parfait glasses. Top each parfait
with a dollop of whipped cream. Serves 8.

Banana-Peanut Parfaits

With a crunchy layer of chocolate and peanuts—

2 bananas, sliced
1 18-ounce can vanilla pudding,
   chilled
   • • •
¼ cup chopped milk chocolate pieces
   or milk chocolate candy bar
¼ cup chopped peanuts

Stir banana slices into pudding. Combine
chopped chocolate and chopped peanuts. In
parfait glasses alternate layers of pudding and
peanut mixture, beginning with pudding and
ending with peanut mixture. (Use about ½ cup
pudding mixture and 1 tablespoon peanut mixture in each parfait.) Makes 6 servings.

Apple Crisp Parfaits

*Tastes like fresh apple pie served with softened
vanilla ice cream—*

1 cup rolled oats
½ cup packed brown sugar
¼ cup butter or margarine, melted
   • • •
1 21-ounce can apple pie filling
¼ teaspoon ground cinnamon
1 quart vanilla ice cream

In 8x8x2-inch baking pan combine oats, brown
sugar, and butter or margarine. Bake at 350°
for 10 minutes (mixture will be soft). Cool and
crumble. Stir together pie filling and cinnamon; divide mixture among 8 parfait glasses.
Top with slightly softened ice cream and the
crumbled oat mixture. Makes 8 servings.

A dessert kids dream about

Banana-Peanut Parfaits *are so easy even the kids* →
*can make them. Keep a can of vanilla pudding in
the refrigerator so they can make these anytime.*

Oranges Piquant

Drain one 11-ounce can chilled mandarin orange sections, reserving 1 tablespoon syrup. In small saucepan combine reserved syrup and 2 tablespoons orange marmalade; heat till marmalade melts. Place drained mandarin oranges in 2 dessert dishes; spoon warm marmalade mixture over. Top with 2 to 3 tablespoons dairy sour cream. Makes 2 servings.

Fruit Compote

Versions given for dieter and non-dieter. Low-calorie serving contains 115 calories —

  1 20-ounce can pineapple chunks
      (juice pack)
1½ cups seedless green grapes
  2 oranges, peeled, sliced, and halved
½ cup shredded coconut
  2 3-ounce packages cream
      cheese, softened
  2 tablespoons brown sugar

Drain pineapple, reserving ¼ cup juice. Combine fruits. Remove ½ cup for dieter; chill. Add coconut to remaining fruit. Chill. Combine cheese and reserved juice. Garnish dieter's portion with 1 tablespoon cheese mixture. Blend sugar into remaining mixture; spoon onto fruit-coconut mixture. Serves 5.

Trim Fruit Compote with cream cheese for the calorie watcher. Others can enjoy a sugared cheese topping and coconut added to the fruit.

Cherry-Orange Compote

  2 medium oranges
  1 16-ounce can pitted dark sweet
      cherries
  1 tablespoon sugar
  2 tablespoons currant jelly
½ cup dry red wine
      Orange Cream

Grate ½ to 1 teaspoon orange peel; set aside. Peel and section oranges. Drain cherries, reserving syrup. In saucepan combine reserved cherry syrup, sugar, and jelly; heat till blended. Stir in wine. Add fruit; chill. Serve with dollops of Orange Cream. Makes 5 servings.
  Orange Cream: Whip 1 cup whipping cream till frothy; add 2 tablespoons sugar and reserved orange peel. Whip till peaks form.

Prune and Apricot Bowl

  2 16-ounce jars stewed prunes (4 cups)
  1 30-ounce can whole apricots
  2 inches stick cinnamon
  3 tablespoons lemon juice
¼ cup rum or brandy

Drain and reserve syrups from prunes and apricots. Combine ½ cup prune syrup and ½ cup apricot syrup; add cinnamon and lemon juice. Simmer 2 to 3 minutes; add rum. Arrange fruits in serving bowl; pour hot syrup over. Serve warm or chilled. Serves 6 to 8.

1-2-3 Fruit Cup

  1 13½-ounce can pineapple tidbits
  1 10-ounce package frozen raspberries,
      thawed
  3 tablespoons orange-flavored breakfast
      drink powder
  1 11-ounce can mandarin orange
      sections, drained

Drain pineapple tidbits and thawed raspberries, reserving syrups. Stir together reserved syrups and breakfast drink powder. Divide pineapple, raspberries, and oranges among 6 sherbets; pour on syrup mixture. Serves 6.

Flaming Pears and Raspberry Sauce

Special dessert for gourmet entertaining—

1½ cups sugar
1½ cups boiling water
1 teaspoon grated lemon peel
2 teaspoons lemon juice
8 pears, peeled
1 10-ounce package frozen raspberries
6 tablespoons orange-flavored liqueur

In Dutch oven combine sugar, water, lemon peel, and lemon juice; simmer 5 minutes. Add pears. Simmer till pears are tender, 10 to 15 minutes. Drain, reserving ¼ cup syrup.

In blender container combine raspberries, reserved syrup, and *2 tablespoons* orange-flavored liqueur. Blend until smooth; strain through sieve. Heat mixture to boiling.

In small saucepan or ladle, warm remaining liqueur. Place warm pears in chafing dish; pour hot raspberry mixture over. Pour warm liqueur over pears and raspberry sauce. Light with match and let flame. Makes 8 servings.

Choco-Scotch-Mallow Fondue

1 14-ounce can sweetened condensed milk
1 7- or 9-ounce jar marshmallow creme
1 6-ounce package butterscotch pieces
4 1-ounce squares unsweetened chocolate
½ cup flaked coconut
½ cup milk
1 teaspoon vanilla
Angel cake cubes or fruit pieces*

In saucepan combine sweetened condensed milk, marshmallow creme, butterscotch pieces, unsweetened chocolate, flaked coconut, milk, and vanilla. Heat through over low heat to melt chocolate and butterscotch; stir thoroughly. Pour into fondue pot; place over fondue burner. (If mixture becomes too thick, stir in a little additional milk.) To serve, spear cubes of angel cake or fruit pieces on fondue fork and dip into fondue. Makes 3½ cups.

*Suggested fruits include pineapple chunks, apple wedges, banana chunks, orange sections, and green or red grapes.

Plums with Custard Sauce

Smooth custard and fruit is 116 calories a serving—

1½ cups skim milk
2 eggs
3 tablespoons sugar
½ teaspoon vanilla
1 16-ounce can calories-reduced purple plums, drained and pitted

In saucepan combine first 4 ingredients and dash salt. Cook and stir over low heat till mixture coats a metal spoon. Remove from heat. Place in pan of cold water; stir a few minutes. Chill. Cut plums in half; place in 6 dessert dishes. Spoon sauce over fruit. Serves 6.

Quick Rice-Raisin Pudding

½ cup uncooked packaged precooked rice
⅓ cup raisins
1 cup nonfat dry milk powder
1 3- or 3¼-ounce package regular vanilla pudding mix

Combine rice, raisins, and 2½ cups water. Bring to boiling; cover and simmer 4 minutes. Stir in milk powder and pudding mix. Cook and stir till thick and bubbly. Serves 4 to 6.

1-2-3 Crème Brûlée

1 3- or 3¼-ounce package regular vanilla pudding mix
1¾ cups milk
½ cup frozen whipped dessert topping, thawed
Brown sugar

Prepare pudding mix according to package directions, *except* use the 1¾ cups milk in place of amount called for. Cool pudding slightly; fold in whipped topping. Spoon into 6 individual custard cups; chill. Sprinkle about *2 teaspoons brown sugar evenly atop each*. Place in shallow ovenproof pan; surround with ice cubes and a little cold water. Broil about 5 inches from heat till bubbly brown crust forms, about 2 minutes. Serve at once. Serves 6.

Shortcut Prune Whip

A scale watcher's special at 109 calories a serving —

2 egg whites
¼ cup sugar
1 4¾-ounce jar strained
        prunes (baby food)
2 teaspoons lemon juice
2 tablespoons chopped pecans

In mixer bowl beat egg whites and dash salt to soft peaks. Gradually add sugar, beating to stiff peaks. Combine prunes and lemon juice. Fold into egg mixture along with pecans. Pile into 4 sherbet glasses. Chill well. Serves 4.

Peach-Caramel Cobbler

Luscious baked dessert pictured on page 74 —

1 29-ounce can peach halves
1 package refrigerated caramel
        Danish rolls with nuts (8 rolls)
¼ cup all-purpose flour
½ teaspoon grated lemon peel
1 7-ounce bottle ginger ale
1 tablespoon butter or margarine

Drain peaches, reserving 1 cup syrup. Cut up peaches and set aside. Crumble sugar-nut mixture from refrigerated caramel rolls into saucepan; add flour, lemon peel, and ¼ teaspoon salt. Stir in ginger ale and reserved syrup; mix well. Cook and stir over medium heat till thickened; stir in butter. Add peaches; bring to boiling. Pour into 8x8x2-inch baking dish. Immediately separate caramel rolls; arrange atop the hot mixture. Bake at 400° till done, 25 to 30 minutes. Makes 8 servings.

Strawberry Meringue Puffs

Beat 2 egg whites and ½ teaspoon vanilla till soft peaks form. Gradually add ½ cup sugar, beating to stiff peaks. Spread mixture on top and sides of 4 sponge cake dessert cups. Place on baking sheet; bake at 450° till golden, about 5 minutes. Remove from oven; fill *center of each* cup with a scoop of strawberry ice cream. Spoon one 10-ounce package frozen strawberries, thawed, over ice cream. Serves 4.

Peanut Butter-Banana Crunch

4 cups sliced bananas
1 tablespoon lemon juice
½ teaspoon ground cinnamon
½ cup all-purpose flour
½ cup packed brown sugar
⅓ cup chunk-style peanut butter
3 tablespoons butter or margarine

Place bananas in 8x1½-inch round baking dish. Add lemon juice and cinnamon, stirring lightly to coat fruit. In small bowl combine flour and brown sugar; cut in peanut butter and butter till mixture is crumbly. Sprinkle over bananas. Bake at 375° for 25 minutes. Top with whipped cream, if desired. Serves 6.

Rhubarb with Meringue Floats

4 cups chopped rhubarb
1¼ cups sugar
3 tablespoons quick-cooking tapioca
2 tablespoons butter or margarine
2 teaspoons grated orange peel
        Red food coloring
2 egg whites
¼ cup sugar

Combine rhubarb, 1¼ cups sugar, tapioca, butter, peel, several drops red food coloring, 2 cups water, and ¼ teaspoon salt. Let stand 5 minutes. Beat egg whites to soft peaks. Gradually add ¼ cup sugar, beating to stiff peaks. Heat rhubarb mixture to boiling; boil 1 minute. Reduce to simmer. Drop meringue by spoonfuls onto hot mixture, forming 6 mounds. Simmer, uncovered, 5 minutes. Serves 6.

Jiffy Peanut Butter Cookies

In large mixer bowl cut 1 cup chunk-style peanut butter and ½ cup shortening into one 2-layer-size yellow cake mix, using low speed of electric mixer. Add 2 eggs and 2 tablespoons water; mix well to form dough. Using 1 tablespoon dough for each cookie, shape into balls. Place on ungreased cookie sheet; flatten each with a fork. Bake at 350° for 15 minutes. Cool thoroughly. Makes about 4½ dozen.

Surprise Pear Bundles

Pear centers are stuffed with cinnamon candies and baked inside a tender, flaky crust—

>   4 pears
>   1 package refrigerated crescent rolls
>   (8 rolls)
>   4 teaspoons red cinnamon candies
>   2 tablespoons sugar

Peel and core pears, leaving whole; set aside. Separate refrigerated dough into 4 rectangles, sealing diagonal perforations. Place one pear upright on each rectangle. Fill *center of each* pear with *1 teaspoon* cinnamon candies; sprinkle *1½ teaspoons* sugar over each. Moisten edges of dough; bring up around pear and seal.

Grease four 6-ounce custard cups or four 2¾-inch muffin cups thoroughly. Place one dough-covered pear in each, seam side up. Bake at 425° for 10 minutes; reduce oven temperature to 350° and bake 20 minutes more. Place each in serving dish; serve warm with cream or ice cream, if desired. Serves 4.

Pears in Chocolate Fluff

Light and fluffy dessert is topped with toasted slivered almonds—

>   1 29-ounce can pear halves
>   ½ cup semisweet chocolate pieces
>   ¼ cup light corn syrup
>   ½ teaspoon vanilla
>   • • •
>   1 cup frozen whipped dessert topping,
>   thawed
>   ¼ cup dairy sour cream
>   ½ cup slivered almonds, toasted

Drain pear halves thoroughly; cut into large pieces and set aside. In small saucepan combine chocolate pieces and corn syrup. Heat, stirring constantly, just till chocolate is melted; stir in vanilla. Cool thoroughly.

Stir together thawed whipped dessert topping and dairy sour cream; fold into cooled chocolate mixture. Add pear pieces and ⅓ *cup* of the slivered toasted almonds. Chill thoroughly. Spoon chilled chocolate mixture into 6 dessert dishes and top with the remaining toasted almonds. Makes 6 servings.

Spiced Butterscotch Pie

Pudding and piecrust mixes make this quick—

>   1 stick piecrust mix
>   ¼ cup finely chopped walnuts
>   ½ teaspoon ground cinnamon
>   ¼ teaspoon ground nutmeg
>   Dash ground ginger
>   1 3¾- or 4-ounce package regular
>   butterscotch pudding mix
>   ½ cup whipping cream

Prepare pastry according to package directions. Roll out and sprinkle with nuts; roll lightly to press nuts in. Fit pastry into 8-inch pie plate; flute edge. Prick bottom and sides with a fork. Bake following package directions; cool.

Add spices to dry pudding mix; cook according to package directions. Cool 5 minutes; turn into pastry shell. Cover surface of pudding with waxed paper. Chill. Remove waxed paper from pie. Whip cream; spread atop pie. Sprinkle with additional chopped nuts, if desired.

Tutti-Frutti Lemon

Serve this one on a hot summer day when you don't want to do any cooking—

>   1 8¾-ounce can pineapple tidbits
>   1 11-ounce can mandarin orange
>   sections
>   1 17-ounce can fruit cocktail
>   ½ cup flaked coconut
>   2 tablespoons lemon juice
>   1 3⅝- or 3¾-ounce package instant
>   lemon pudding mix
>   • • •
>   2 bananas
>   Frozen whipped dessert topping,
>   thawed

In large mixing bowl combine undrained pineapple tidbits, undrained mandarin orange sections, undrained fruit cocktail, flaked coconut, and lemon juice. Sprinkle the instant lemon pudding mix over fruits and toss lightly to combine; chill thoroughly. Just before serving, peel and slice bananas. Fold bananas into lemon-fruit mixture. Serve in dessert dishes or sherbets; top with dollops of the thawed whipped dessert topping. Makes 10 servings.

Strawberry-Banana Dessert

Even non-dieters will enjoy eating this pretty, refreshing dessert at only 116 calories a serving—

  1 3½-ounce package soft-style
    strawberry whipped dessert mix
  1 cup low-calorie lemon-lime
    carbonated beverage
      • • •
  1 large banana
  1 teaspoon sugar
  ½ cup plain yogurt

Prepare strawberry whipped dessert mix according to package directions, *except* use carbonated beverage in place of milk and water called for. Mash *half* the banana with fork; slice remaining banana and set aside. Fold mashed banana into whipped mixture. Stir sugar into yogurt; fold into whipped mixture along with sliced banana. Chill. Serves 6.

Citrus Sauce

This refreshing fruit sauce makes a great topping for waffles, ice cream, or cake slices—

  ½ cup sugar
  2 tablespoons cornstarch
    Dash salt
  ¾ cup water
      • • •
  ½ teaspoon grated orange peel
  ½ cup orange juice
  ½ teaspoon grated lemon peel
  1 tablespoon lemon juice
  1 tablespoon butter or margarine

In saucepan combine sugar, cornstarch, and salt. Stir in water; bring to boiling. Cook and stir till thickened and bubbly. Stir in grated orange peel, orange juice, lemon peel, lemon juice, and butter or margarine; heat through. Serve warm. Makes 1⅓ cups.

Bake a batch of Ginger Waffles or quickly heat frozen ones, and offer tangy Citrus Sauce or Blueberry-Nutmeg Sauce as toppers. Have a bowl of fluffy whipped cream or ice cream on hand for the crowning touch.

Ginger Waffles

Good topped with ice cream, too—

Preheat waffle baker. In bowl combine 3 cups finely crushed gingersnaps, 4 teaspoons baking powder, and ½ teaspoon salt. Combine 3 beaten egg yolks, 1 cup milk, and ¼ cup butter or margarine, melted; stir into crumb mixture.

Beat 3 egg whites till stiff; fold into egg yolk mixture just till combined. Bake in preheated waffle baker. Serve warm with Citrus Sauce, if desired. Makes 14.

Blueberry-Nutmeg Sauce

- **1 cup sugar**
- **2 tablespoons cornstarch**
- **½ teaspoon freshly grated nutmeg**
- **1 10-ounce package frozen blueberries, thawed**
- **3 tablespoons lemon juice**

In saucepan combine sugar, cornstarch, nutmeg, and dash salt. Gradually stir in 1 cup water; cook and stir till thick and bubbly. Stir in blueberries and lemon juice. Heat through.

Cake and Frosting Alaska

- **1 package 1-layer-size chocolate cake mix**
- **1 quart brick or 2 pint bricks cherry-nut or strawberry ice cream**
- **1 package fluffy white frosting mix (for 2-layer cake)**

Prepare cake mix according to package directions; pour into greased and floured 9x9x2-inch baking pan. Bake according to package directions. Cool 10 minutes; remove from pan. Cool thoroughly. Trim cake so it will be 1 inch larger on all sides than brick of ice cream; place on wooden cutting board. (Keep ice cream frozen till ready to use.) Prepare frosting mix according to package directions. Center ice cream on cake. Working very quickly, spread frosting over ice cream and cake, sealing to edges of cake all around. Bake at 500° till meringue is golden, 4 to 5 minutes. Serve immediately. Makes 8 to 10 servings.

Banana-Date Dessert

Date-nut treat has 133 calories a serving—

- **1 egg**
- **2 tablespoons sugar**
- **2 tablespoons skim milk**
- **1 teaspoon lemon juice**
- **½ banana, chopped**
- **1 cup whipped low-calorie dessert topping**
- **6 ½-inch slices canned date-nut roll**

In small saucepan beat egg, sugar, and milk. Cook and stir over low heat till slightly thickened. Stir in lemon juice. Cool thoroughly. Stir in chopped banana. Fold in whipped topping. Chill. To serve, top date-nut slices with topping. Makes 6 servings.

Date Crumb Cake

- **1 14-ounce package date bar mix**
- **2 cups packaged biscuit mix**
- **3 tablespoons sugar**
- **⅔ cup milk**
- **1 slightly beaten egg**
- **2 tablespoons cooking oil**

Prepare date filling and crumb mixture from date bar mix according to package directions. Pat *1½ cups* of the crumb mixture on bottom of ungreased 9x9x2-inch baking pan. In mixing bowl combine biscuit mix and sugar. Blend milk, egg, and oil; stir into biscuit mix-sugar mixture till well mixed. Spread *half* of the mixture over crumbs in pan. Top with date filling; spread remaining biscuit mixture carefully over filling. Sprinkle with remaining crumb mixture. Bake at 375° till done, about 25 minutes. Serve warm or cool.

Cinnamon-Pecan Slices

Cut 1 roll refrigerated sugar cookie dough into ¼-inch slices. Combine ½ cup chopped pecans and ¾ teaspoon ground cinnamon. Dip tops of cookies in pecan-cinnamon mixture; arrange on ungreased cookie sheet. Bake at 375° till lightly browned, 8 to 10 minutes. Makes about 3½ dozen cookies.

Desserts on Call

Coffee Angel Pie

Heat the raisin sauce just before serving—

   2 egg whites
   ½ teaspoon vanilla
   ¼ teaspoon salt
   ¼ teaspoon cream of tartar
   ½ cup granulated sugar
   ½ cup finely chopped pecans
   • • •
   1 pint coffee ice cream
   1 pint vanilla ice cream
   • • •
   Caramel-Raisin Sauce

In large mixing bowl beat together egg whites, vanilla, salt, and cream of tartar till soft peaks form. Very gradually beat in the granulated sugar till very stiff peaks form and sugar is completely dissolved. Carefully fold in the finely chopped pecans. Spread the egg white mixture in a well-buttered 9-inch pie plate, building up the sides with a spoon to form a shell. Bake at 275° for 1 hour. Turn off heat and let dry in oven (door closed) for 1 hour more. Cool. Pile scoops of coffee ice cream and vanilla ice cream into cooled meringue shell; freeze. Let the pie stand for 20 minutes at room temperature before serving. Serve the pie with warm Caramel-Raisin Sauce.

Caramel-Raisin Sauce: In small saucepan melt 3 tablespoons butter or margarine over low heat. Stir in 1 cup packed brown sugar, one 6-ounce can evaporated milk (⅔ cup), and dash salt. Cook and stir brown sugar mixture over medium-low heat just till mixture boils. Remove sauce from heat; stir in ½ cup light raisins and 1 teaspoon vanilla. Cool mixture slightly. Makes 1⅓ cups sauce.

For extra-special occasions

← *Elegant* Coffee Angel Pie *waits in the freezer. The pecan meringue and ice cream pie is made ahead; just before serving, warm sauce and spoon over.*

Peach Cream Dessert

Airy dessert contains 97 calories per serving—

   2 envelopes unflavored
      gelatin
   ⅓ cup sugar
      Dash salt
   1 16-ounce can low-calorie peach
      halves
   1¼ cups cold water
   1 6-ounce can frozen red Hawaiian
      fruit punch concentrate
   1 cup frozen whipped dessert topping,
      thawed

DIET DESSERT • DIET DESSERT

In saucepan combine gelatin, sugar, and salt. Drain peaches, reserving juice. Cut up peaches and set aside. Add water to reserved juice to make 1 cup; stir into gelatin mixture. Cook and stir over low heat till gelatin dissolves. Stir in cold water and punch concentrate. Chill till partially set. Whip gelatin mixture till light and fluffy. Fold in dessert topping and peaches. Turn into 7½-cup mold. Chill till firm, 4 to 5 hours or overnight. Serves 12.

Confetti Freeze

Tiny assorted marshmallows polka dot the filling layered between rich chocolate crumbs—

   1¼ cups finely crushed chocolate
      wafers (23 cookies)
   ¼ cup butter or margarine, melted
   2 2-ounce packages dessert
      topping mix
   3 cups tiny assorted flavored
      marshmallows
   ¾ cup coarsely crushed buttermints

Combine crushed wafers and butter. Reserve 3 tablespoons crumb mixture; press remaining into 9x9x2-inch baking pan. Bake at 350° for 10 minutes; cool. Prepare topping mix according to package directions; fold in marshmallows and mints. Spread over crust; sprinkle reserved crumbs over. Freeze. Makes 8 servings.

Peanut Butter Tortoni

Easy, individual servings to make ahead—

⅓ cup creamy peanut butter
¼ cup sugar
1 teaspoon instant coffee powder
1 teaspoon vanilla
1 egg white
1 tablespoon sugar
• • •
1 cup whipping cream
½ cup finely crushed coconut cookies
⅓ cup chopped peanuts

Blend together peanut butter, ¼ cup sugar, coffee powder, and vanilla. Beat egg white till soft peaks form. Gradually beat in 1 tablespoon sugar till stiff peaks form. Fold beaten egg white into peanut butter mixture.

Whip cream just till soft peaks form. Combine crushed cookies and peanuts; fold *half* into the peanut butter mixture. Fold in whipped cream. Spoon into 6 paper bake cups or individual serving dishes. Sprinkle with remaining crumb-peanut mixture. Freeze firm. Serves 6.

Blueberry Marble Dessert

Tangy dessert contains only 105 calories a serving—

2 4-serving envelopes low-calorie
  lemon-flavored gelatin
1 cup boiling water
1⅔ cups cold water
½ of a 6-ounce can frozen
  lemonade concentrate
½ cup sugar
1 8-ounce carton plain yogurt (1 cup)
1 9-ounce package frozen unsweetened
  blueberries, thawed (1¾ cups)

Dissolve gelatin in boiling water. Stir in cold water and lemonade concentrate. Stir sugar into yogurt. Slowly blend *1 cup* gelatin mixture into yogurt. Chill both mixtures till partially set. (Plain mixture sets up faster, so start chilling yogurt mixture first.)

Rinse and drain blueberries. Fold into plain gelatin mixture. Layer fruit mixture and yogurt mixture in 5½-cup mold. Cut through with spatula to marble. Chill till firm, several hours or overnight. Makes 9 servings.

Mocha-Toffee Parfaits

1 3- or 3¼-ounce package regular
  vanilla pudding mix
1 tablespoon instant coffee powder
1¾ cups milk
½ cup semisweet chocolate pieces
1 6-ounce can evaporated milk
1 1⅛-ounce chocolate-coated English
  toffee bar, coarsely crushed
Whipped cream

In medium saucepan combine pudding mix and coffee powder; gradually stir in milk till mixture is blended. Cook over medium heat, stirring constantly, till mixture comes to boiling. Remove from heat and cover surface of pudding with waxed paper; cool and chill.

In small saucepan combine chocolate pieces and evaporated milk. Cook and stir over low heat till mixture boils and chocolate is melted. Cool and chill.

Remove paper from pudding mixture; spoon *half* the mixture into 4 parfait glasses. Top with *half* the chocolate sauce and *half* the crushed candy. Repeat layering with remaining pudding mixture and chocolate sauce. Top parfaits with dollops of whipped cream and remaining crushed candy. Makes 4 servings.

Frosty Butterscotch Squares

Butterscotch frosting is part of flavorful filling—

¾ cup finely crushed graham crackers
¼ cup sugar
¼ cup butter or margarine, melted
1 can ready-to-spread butterscotch
  frosting
1 cup cream-style cottage cheese
1 cup dairy sour cream

Combine crushed graham crackers, sugar, and butter or margarine; mix well. Press firmly and evenly in bottom of 9x9x2-inch baking pan. Bake at 350° for 10 minutes; cool.

In small mixer bowl combine frosting, cottage cheese, and sour cream. Beat on high speed of electric mixer till blended, about 3 minutes. Pour into crumb-lined pan. Freeze till firm, at least 6 hours. Garnish with walnut halves, if desired. Makes 8 to 10 servings.

Rhubarb Torte

An excellent use for fresh rhubarb—

> 1 cup sugar
> 3 tablespoons cornstarch
> 4 cups sliced rhubarb
> ½ cup water
>   Few drops red food coloring
>   Graham Cracker Crust
> ½ cup whipping cream
> 1½ cups tiny marshmallows
> 1 3⅝- or 3¾-ounce package
>   instant vanilla pudding mix

Combine sugar and cornstarch; stir in rhubarb and water. Cook and stir till thickened. Reduce heat; cook 2 to 3 minutes. Add food coloring. Spread over Graham Cracker Crust. Cool.

Whip cream; fold in marshmallows. Spoon over rhubarb mixture. Prepare pudding mix according to package directions; spread over all. Sprinkle with reserved crust. Chill. Serves 9.

Graham Cracker Crust: Combine 1 cup finely crushed graham crackers, ¼ cup melted butter, and 2 tablespoons sugar; reserve 2 tablespoons mixture. Pat remainder in 9x9x2-inch baking pan. Bake at 350° for 10 minutes. Cool.

Butterscotch Crunch Squares

Chocolate ice cream is the filling—

> 1 cup all-purpose flour
> ¼ cup quick-cooking rolled oats
> ¼ cup packed brown sugar
> ½ cup butter or margarine
> ½ cup chopped nuts
> 1 12-ounce jar butterscotch or caramel
>   ice cream topping
> 1 quart chocolate ice cream

Combine flour, oats, and brown sugar; cut in butter or margarine till mixture resembles coarse crumbs. Stir in nuts. Pat mixture into 13x9x2-inch baking pan. Bake at 400° for 15 minutes. Stir while warm to crumble; cool.

Spread *half* the crumbs in 9x9x2-inch baking pan; drizzle *about half* the ice cream topping over crumbs in pan. Stir ice cream to soften; spoon carefully into pan. Drizzle with remaining topping; sprinkle with remaining crumbs. Freeze till firm. Makes 8 servings.

Frozen whipped cream toppers

To freeze dollops of whipped cream, drop heaping spoonfuls on chilled baking sheet, swirling the tops with tip of spoon. Then place the baking sheet in the freezer. When frozen, lift mounds from baking sheet with spatula; put them in a plastic bag. Seal tightly and store till ready to use. Frozen whipped cream mounds will stay fresh for 3 months. Thaw the toppers in the refrigerator about 45 minutes before using them to garnish desserts.

Raspberry-Angel Dessert

Perfect for a party at 99 calories a serving—

> 1 4-serving envelope low-calorie
>   raspberry-flavored gelatin
> 1½ cups boiling water
> ½ cup unsweetened pineapple juice
> ½ cup reconstituted nonfat dry milk
> 1 2-ounce package dessert
>   topping mix
> 1 teaspoon vanilla
> 3 cups angel cake cubes

Dissolve gelatin in boiling water; stir in pineapple juice. Chill till partially set. Using the reconstituted nonfat dry milk, prepare dessert topping mix following package directions, *except* increase the vanilla to 1 teaspoon. Fold gelatin and angel cake cubes into 1 cup of the topping. Turn into 10x6x2-inch dish. Chill till almost firm. Frost with remaining topping; chill till firm. Makes 10 servings.

Jade Cream Mold

Prepare one 2-ounce package dessert topping mix according to package directions. Stir 1 quart vanilla ice cream and 1 pint lime sherbet to soften, then stir together along with dessert topping. Swirl in ¼ cup green crème de menthe. Turn into 5- or 6-cup mold. Freeze till firm, 6 hours or overnight. Garnish with fresh mint sprigs and frosted grapes, if desired. Serves 8.

Angel-Sherbet Supreme

   1 10-inch angel cake
   1 quart or 2 pints pineapple sherbet
   ¼ cup green crème de menthe
   1 cup whipping cream
   2 tablespoons sugar
   2 or 3 drops green food coloring

Slice 1 inch off top of cake; set aside. Cut down into cake, removing interior and leaving wall 1 inch thick on all sides. Stir sherbet just till softened. Swirl crème de menthe into sherbet; quickly spoon into hollowed portion of cake. Replace top section of cake. Wrap and freeze till serving time.

   To serve, place cake on serving plate. Whip cream, sugar, and green food coloring just till soft peaks form. Use whipped mixture to frost top and sides of cake. Serve immediately.

Orange Icebox Cake

   ½ cup sugar
   1 envelope unflavored gelatin
   ¼ teaspoon salt
   2 egg yolks
   ¾ cup milk
   1 teaspoon grated orange peel
   ¼ cup orange juice
      Few drops yellow food coloring
         • • •
   2 egg whites
   ¼ cup sugar
   ½ cup whipping cream
   12 ladyfingers, split

In saucepan mix ½ cup sugar, gelatin, and salt. Beat yolks with milk; add to gelatin mixture. Cook and stir over low heat till gelatin dissolves and mixture is slightly thickened. Add peel, juice, and food coloring. Chill till partially set. Beat whites till soft peaks form; gradually add ¼ cup sugar, beating till stiff peaks form. Whip cream. Beat gelatin mixture till frothy; fold in egg whites and whipped cream. Line 9x5x3-inch loaf pan with waxed paper; then line with ladyfingers. Fill with gelatin mixture; chill till set, at least 4 hours. Garnish with additional whipped cream, if desired. Makes 8 to 10 servings.

Apricot-Wafer Dessert

   1½ cups dried apricots
   ½ cup granulated sugar
   1½ cups crushed vanilla wafers
   3 tablespoons butter, melted
   ½ cup butter or margarine, softened
   1½ cups sifted powdered sugar
   2 slightly beaten eggs
   1 cup whipping cream

In saucepan cover apricots with water. Bring to boiling. Simmer till very tender, about 20 minutes. Drain. Sieve. Stir in granulated sugar; set aside. Combine wafers and melted butter. Reserve ½ cup crumb mixture; press remaining mixture in bottom of 10x6x2-inch baking dish. Cream the ½ cup butter and powdered sugar till fluffy. Beat in eggs. Spoon atop wafer crust. Spread sieved apricots over butter mixture. Whip cream. Spread over apricot layer. Sprinkle with reserved crumbs. Chill 12 hours or overnight. Remove from refrigerator 15 minutes before serving. Serves 8.

Fruitcake Soufflés

Delightful, tiny servings shown on page 75 —

   1 3- or 3¼-ounce package regular
      vanilla pudding mix
   1 envelope unflavored gelatin
   3 cups milk
   ¼ teaspoon rum flavoring
   1½ cups crumbled fruitcake
   1 4½-ounce carton frozen whipped
      dessert topping, thawed
      Ground nutmeg
   6 maraschino cherries

In saucepan combine pudding mix and gelatin; stir in milk. Cook and stir till mixture comes to a boil; remove from heat and stir in rum flavoring. Chill till partially set. Fold in crumbled fruitcake and *half* of the whipped topping. Secure waxed paper collars around 6 ½- or ⅔- cup individual soufflé dishes. Spoon in fruitcake mixture. Sprinkle with nutmeg. Chill till set, at least 2 hours. To serve, remove collars; top each with a dollop of remaining whipped dessert topping and a maraschino cherry. Makes 6 servings.

Lemon Layer Wedges

    Pastry for 2-crust pie
 1 cup sugar
 1 envelope unflavored gelatin
 3 slightly beaten eggs
 1 teaspoon grated lemon peel
 ⅓ cup lemon juice
 2 tablespoons butter or margarine
 ½ cup whipping cream

Roll *half* the pastry to ⅛-inch thickness. Fit into 9-inch pie plate. Flute edges; prick bottom and sides with fork. Bake at 450° for 10 to 12 minutes. Divide remaining pastry in half. Roll *each half* to ⅛-inch thickness; trim one to an 8-inch circle, the other to an 8¾-inch circle. Place on baking sheet; prick. Bake at 450° for 8 to 10 minutes; cool.

Combine sugar and gelatin; add eggs, lemon peel, juice, butter, and 1¼ cups water. Cook, stirring constantly, over low heat till mixture thickens, about 10 minutes. Chill till mixture mounds. Whip cream; fold into lemon mixture. Place *1 cup* of the filling into baked pastry shell; cover with the 8-inch pastry round. Repeat with *1 cup* lemon filling and the 8¾-inch pastry round. Top with remaining filling. Chill till set, 3 to 4 hours. Garnish with additional whipped cream, if desired.

Candy Bar Pie

 1⅓ cups grated coconut
   2 tablespoons butter or margarine,
       melted
   1 teaspoon instant coffee powder
   1 7½-ounce milk chocolate candy bar
       with almonds, broken
   4 cups frozen whipped dessert topping,
       thawed

Combine coconut and butter; press into 8-inch pie plate. Bake at 325° till coconut is golden, about 10 minutes. Cool thoroughly.

In small saucepan dissolve coffee powder in 2 tablespoons water; add chocolate bar. Stir chocolate mixture over low heat till melted; cool. Fold in whipped dessert topping; pile into coconut crust. Chill in freezer several hours or overnight (it will not freeze solid).

Grasshopper Pie

Crème de menthe and crème de cacao combine in this satisfying mint pie—

    Chocolate wafers
 1 7- or 9-ounce jar marshmallow creme
 2 tablespoons green crème de menthe
 2 tablespoons white crème de cacao
 1 cup whipping cream

Line bottom of 9-inch pie plate with cookies, filling in spaces between with pieces of cookie. Line sides of pie plate with half-cookies. Set aside. In mixer bowl combine marshmallow creme, crème de menthe, and crème de cacao. Beat on high speed of electric mixer till fluffy, about 1 minute. Whip cream; fold into marshmallow mixture. Spoon filling into cookie crust. Freeze 8 hours or overnight (it will not freeze solid). Garnish with additional whipped cream and chocolate curls, if desired.

Creamy Candy Bar Pie *makes the perfect ending to any occasion. The smooth filling chills to just the right consistency in the freezer for serving.*

Basic Homemade Ice Cream

¾ cup sugar
1½ teaspoons unflavored gelatin
4 cups light cream
1 slightly beaten egg
2 teaspoons vanilla
Dash salt

In saucepan combine sugar and gelatin. Stir in *2 cups* light cream. Heat and stir over low heat till gelatin dissolves. Slowly stir a small amount of hot mixture into egg; return to remaining hot mixture. Cook and stir till slightly thickened, about 1 minute. Chill. Add remaining cream, vanilla, and salt. Freeze in ice-cream freezer according to manufacturer's directions. Makes 1½ quarts.

Strawberry Ice Cream: Prepare Basic Homemade Ice Cream, *except* decrease sugar to ½ cup and decrease vanilla to 1 teaspoon. Combine 1 quart strawberries and ¾ cup sugar; crush berries and stir into chilled mixture.

Cherry-Nut Ice Cream: Prepare Basic Homemade Ice Cream, *except* decrease vanilla to 1 teaspoon. Add ⅓ cup chopped walnuts and ⅓ cup chopped maraschino cherries with 1 tablespoon cherry juice to the chilled mixture.

Chocolate-Nut Ice Cream: Prepare Basic Homemade Ice Cream, *except* increase sugar to 1 cup. Add three 1-ounce squares unsweetened chocolate, cut up, to gelatin mixture. Decrease vanilla to 1 teaspoon and add ½ cup toasted slivered almonds to chilled mixture.

Peppermint Ice Cream: Prepare Basic Homemade Ice Cream, *except* add 1 cup crushed peppermint candies to hot gelatin mixture; stir till melted. Decrease vanilla to 1 teaspoon. Stir ¼ cup coarsely crushed peppermint candies into frozen ice cream.

Summertime treat for everybody

Be ready for volunteer tasters when you make Basic Homemade Ice Cream *or its variations:* Cherry-Nut, Chocolate-Nut, Peppermint, *and* Strawberry.

Fresh Strawberry Ice Cream

You can make this one in the refrigerator—

1 envelope unflavored gelatin
2 well-beaten egg yolks
2 cups whipping cream
1 pint strawberries, crushed (1½ cups)
¾ cup sugar
1½ teaspoons vanilla
10 to 12 drops red food coloring
2 egg whites
¼ cup sugar

Soften gelatin in ¼ cup cold water; dissolve over hot water. Combine next 6 ingredients and ¼ teaspoon salt. Add gelatin; mix well. Turn into one 6-cup or two 3-cup refrigerator trays; freeze. Beat egg whites to soft peaks. Gradually add ¼ cup sugar, beating to stiff peaks. Break frozen strawberry mixture into chunks; beat till fluffy. Fold in beaten egg whites. Return to trays; freeze. Serves 8 to 10.

Choco-Mo Ice Cream

This cool molasses and chocolate chip ice cream is pictured on page 74—

1 tablespoon cornstarch
1 14½-ounce can evaporated milk
3 egg yolks
¼ cup light molasses
3 egg whites
¼ cup sugar
½ cup semisweet chocolate pieces,
   finely chopped

Combine cornstarch and ⅔ cup water in saucepan. Stir in evaporated milk. Cook and stir till mixture boils. Beat egg yolks till light. Stir small amount hot mixture into egg yolks. Return to remaining hot mixture in saucepan. Cook and stir till mixture is *almost boiling.* Stir in molasses and dash salt; chill.

Beat egg whites till soft peaks form. Gradually add sugar, beating till stiff peaks form. Fold into molasses mixture.

Turn into 11x7½x1½-inch pan. Freeze till firm. Break in chunks and place in bowl; beat till smooth with electric mixer. Fold in chopped chocolate pieces. Return to cold pan. Freeze till firm. Makes 8 to 10 servings.

Freezing ice cream

Pour ice cream mixture into ice cream freezer can till ⅔ full. Fit can into freezer. If using electric ice-cream freezer, follow manufacturer's directions.

Adjust dasher and cover. Pack crushed ice and rock salt around can, using 6 parts ice to 1 part salt. Turn dasher slowly till ice partially melts and forms brine—add more ice and salt to maintain ice level. Turn handle constantly till crank turns hard. Remove ice to below lid of can; remove lid and dasher.

To ripen ice cream: Plug opening in lid. Cover can with several thicknesses of waxed paper or foil; replace lid. Pack more ice and salt (use 4 parts ice to 1 part salt) around can. Cover with heavy cloth or newspapers. Let ripen 4 hours.

Frosty Orange Freeze

Icy orange-flavored treat contains only 53 calories a serving—

In large refrigerator tray combine ½ cup fresh orange juice and one 12-ounce bottle lemon-lime carbonated beverage. Freeze till crystals form on bottom; stir. Freeze till slushy. Pour into chilled small mixer bowl; quickly beat till smooth. Return to tray; freeze. Scoop into sherbets. Place 4 orange slices, peeled, quartered, and chilled around edges. Serves 4.

Lime Sherbet Surprise

Buttermilk is the surprise in this 82 calories a serving treat—

Combine one 3-ounce package lime-flavored gelatin and ½ cup sugar; dissolve in 1½ cups boiling water. Stir in 1 cup buttermilk, 1 teaspoon grated lemon peel, and 3 tablespoons lemon juice. Turn into 4-cup refrigerator tray; freeze firm. Break into chunks; beat smooth with electric mixer. Beat 1 egg white till stiff peaks form. Fold into gelatin mixture. Freeze in tray till firm. Makes 10 servings.

Peppermint Ice Cream Roll

Single serving shown on page 75 —

    4 egg yolks
    ¼ cup granulated sugar
    ½ teaspoon vanilla
    4 egg whites
    ½ cup granulated sugar
    ⅔ cup sifted cake flour
    ¼ cup unsweetened cocoa powder
    1 teaspoon baking powder
    Powdered sugar
    1 quart peppermint ice cream
    ¼ cup crushed peppermint candy
    1 cup frozen whipped dessert topping, thawed

In mixer bowl beat egg yolks till thick and lemon-colored; gradually beat in ¼ cup granulated sugar. Add vanilla. In mixer bowl beat egg whites till soft peaks form; gradually add the ½ cup sugar, beating to stiff peaks. Fold yolk mixture into whites. Sift together flour, cocoa, baking powder, and ¼ teaspoon salt; fold into egg mixture. Spread batter evenly in greased and floured 15½x10½x1-inch jelly roll pan. Bake at 375° for 10 to 12 minutes.

Immediately loosen sides and turn out onto towel sprinkled with sifted powdered sugar. Starting at narrow end, roll cake and towel together; cool. Unroll; top with ice cream softened to spreading consistency. Roll up and freeze. To serve, stir crushed candy into dessert topping. Cut cake; top each serving with topping mixture. Garnish with additional crushed candy, if desired. Makes 10 servings.

Choco-Mint Freeze

In saucepan combine one 3- or 3¼-ounce package *regular* vanilla pudding mix and ½ cup sugar; stir in 2 cups milk. Cook and stir till thickened and bubbly. Remove from heat; stir in ¼ teaspoon peppermint extract and ¼ teaspoon green or red food coloring. Cover surface with waxed paper and chill. Stir in ½ cup semisweet mint-flavored chocolate pieces, chopped. Whip 1 cup whipping cream just till peaks form; fold into pudding mixture. Turn into 4-cup refrigerator tray; freeze till firm. Spoon into sherbets. Makes 8 servings.

Ribbon-Layered Lemon Pie

Remove from freezer 10 minutes before serving —

    ¼ cup butter or margarine
    ¾ cup sugar
    ⅓ cup lemon juice
    Dash salt
    3 slightly beaten eggs
    1 pint vanilla ice cream, softened
    1 9-inch Graham Cracker Crust (see recipe, page 51)
    1 pint vanilla ice cream, softened

In medium saucepan melt butter or margarine; stir in sugar, lemon juice, and salt. Cook and stir till sugar dissolves. Pour *half* of hot mixture into eggs. Return all to saucepan. Cook, stirring constantly, till thickened; chill. Place 1 pint ice cream in Graham Cracker Crust. Spread with *half* of the chilled lemon sauce. Freeze pie till firm, several hours. Repeat layers with remaining ice cream and lemon sauce. Freeze till firm. Garnish with fresh strawberries, if desired.

Ice Cream Sundae Mold

Two-layered ice cream treat with chocolate sauce —

    ¼ cup flaked coconut, toasted
    1½ teaspoons brandy flavoring
    1 quart vanilla ice cream, softened
    • • •
    1 quart coffee ice cream, softened
    ¼ cup slivered almonds, toasted
    Fudgy Chocolate Sauce

Stir coconut and brandy flavoring into vanilla ice cream; turn into a 6-cup mold and freeze firm. Stir together coffee ice cream and almonds; spoon into mold atop vanilla layer. Freeze firm, about 5 hours.

Unmold onto serving plate. Drizzle with Fudgy Chocolate Sauce; sprinkle with additional almonds, if desired. Pass remaining sauce. Makes 10 to 12 servings.

Fudgy Chocolate Sauce: In saucepan combine one 6-ounce package semisweet chocolate pieces and ⅔ cup light corn syrup; cook and stir over low heat till chocolate melts. Remove from heat; cool. Gradually stir in one 6-ounce can evaporated milk (⅔ cup).

INDEX

A-B